SUSIE'S STORY

THOMAS ERROL WASDIN

Wingspan Press

Published in the United States and the United Kingdom
by WingSpan Press, Livermore, CA

The WingSpan name, logo and colophon are the trademarks of
WingSpan Publishing.

ISBN 978-1-63683-074-2 (pbk.)
ISBN 978-1-63683-938-7 (ebk.)

Printed in the United States of America

www.wingspanpress.com

Cover Photo: Ray Baldino Photography Studios, Indialantic, Fl.

Leonard, Suzy Fleming. "Living with Alzheimer's: Longtime Cocoa philanthropist's light dims as the disease sets in," Florida Today, 18 September 2023, used by permission.

We've watched you slowly shrink before our eyes,
Pale, lethargic and restless,
Our hearts have melted as we felt helpless to make things right,
Knowing what you're going through but unable to share or take the burden from you,
Yet, we have been inspired by your courage and determination,
Thrilled by your certainty that better days are ahead,
We worry about the feelings you are hiding while alone with your thoughts,
Yet you continue to think of others,
Determined that your burden will not burden others,
Maintaining a façade of good cheer and bonhomie,
We cannot relieve your suffering,
But we can suffer our feelings of despair and anger,
That such a person should bear this betrayal by her body in the prime of life,
We can only offer words of encouragement and hope,
And our undying love.

Anonymous

INTRODUCTION

My wife and best friend, Susie, is one of the more than 6.7 million Americans suffering from Alzheimer's. Over the past ten years, I have watched this once dynamic and vibrant woman disappear before my eyes, replaced by a smiling and complacent lady with no memory of persons, places, or events from the past. Even the occasional flashes of memory are disjointed and unconnected to reality. Physically, there has been little change for Susie, and frequent medical checkups pronounce her as healthy as any person her age, but the Susie I knew and loved is gone forever. Sadly, she is not alone in suffering from this dreaded disease.

Medical authorities now predict that 1 in 9 Americans over 65, male and female, have Alzheimer's and the number who suffer is expected to grow to more than 14 million by 2060. In addition, there are approximately 7 million who suffer from dementia, which shares many of the same symptoms, and that number is predicted to grow to 9 million by 2030 and to 12 million by 2040. Both Alzheimer's and dementia are medical conditions that have similar underlying causes. Although many millions of dollars have been expended on trying to find a cure for these diseases, progress has been slow with success still very far away.

I decided to write Susie's story for several reasons. First, I want to let people know what a remarkable woman she has been in the past. Her achievements as a wife, companion, and mother were exceptional. Her steadfast love and care for me when I was suffering from the onslaught of trigeminal neuralgia were important factors in my recovery; I can do no less for her now. This book is a celebration of her life.

Second, Susie's medical condition is not one she suffers alone. Her absence, both physically and mentally, has had an impact on her family and friends, particularly on me. Susie is now in the end stage of her illness, unable to move or care for herself. She is not forgotten and has been included in family activities and some social events until quite recently, and we have each developed coping strategies for how we interact with her and how she interacts with us. It is not an easy task but a necessary one. This is also the story of how we cope with her loss.

Third, I want to share with other caregivers my experiences in adjusting my life and activities as a husband of a slowly fading Alzheimer's patient. I also want to learn from them how to cope with the dilemmas created by the conflict of providing care and carrying on a normal existence—for example, to what extent is my life curtailed by her illness? I also want to encourage other caregivers to take advantage of the many support groups, community resources, and government programs that have been created to alleviate the "going it alone" syndrome. I have used these resources and I also urge others to do so. I have appended a short list of readily available resources at the end of this book.

Last, I want to encourage my fellow caregivers to be open about discussing all aspects of this disease and its impact on them. To attempt to deal with a loved one with Alzheimer's or dementia alone is to invite your own mental and emotional problems. Remember, rule number one is that as a caregiver, your wellbeing is of primary importance.

I would like to thank Nick Wynne for his help with writing this book. He has been a friend and a coffee klatch member for many years.

I would also like to thank the many family members and friends who shared their memories of the real Susie. Some of them have known her entire life and have willingly shared their recollections for inclusion in this book. Their memories so lovingly portray this remarkable woman, my wife.

I also want to thank Susie for giving me forty years of love, excitement, and commitment. Though things have changed in the past five years due to Alzheimer's, nothing has changed about or with my love for her.

Tom Wasdin
August 2025

PREFACE

My name is Susie Thortsen Wasdin and this is my story. Although I am now unable to voice my own memories and recollections, I have left a legacy of newspaper articles and television interviews during my earlier years which served as the basis for my story. My story is written in the first person and it is as if I am speaking for myself.

I will not be able to read and understand this book, although I hope it will help others who suffer like me. I have Alzheimer's.

I knew what was happening to me six or seven years ago. Things that were commonplace became mysteries, and people I once knew very well became ghostly figures appearing in familiar places but no longer in the context of my frame of reference. Small things that I would have once dismissed as unimportant became minor irritants to me. I would display my irritation, and that was not who I was. While I once played an important role in the affairs of our company, I understood that my participation was coming to an end, and I slowly withdrew from my corporate responsibilities.

Once I became aware of the devastating progress of this disease; I asked Tom to go public with my illness in the hope that people would benefit from my story. He did, and our friend Susie Fleming Leonard published a nice article in *Florida Today*. Maybe someone out there will find the article helpful and a copy of this article is included at the end of this book. I also asked Tom to promise that I would remain at home, and that I would not be put in an assisted living facility where so often people are warehoused and forgotten. My darling Tom has lived up to this promise.

As my illness progressed, I realized that I would have to gradually withdraw from everyone. While I still could, I wanted to ensure that my loved ones understood that, while they might want to help, I had to take this journey alone. I let them know that I wanted them to live their lives to the fullest, doing what they would have done normally, but without forgetting about me. Just because I was curtailing my public life did not mean that they should change theirs. My death sentence should not and could not be theirs.

I am now in the netherworld of forgetfulness, unable to speak, move, or feed myself. I have become dependent on other people for the basics of life. My world, once filled with promising new adventures each day, has shrunk to two rooms in our condo. I am helpless to do anything. My days are filled with fleeting images of my past life, mostly pleasant ones and ones that make me smile, and the helpful ladies that take care of me. I could not ask for better care and I am thankful for that.

I am always happy to see the nice man who comes and sits by my side and talks to me each day. He says he is Tom my husband. Sadly, I no longer remember what a husband is, but I listened to him and his voice brings me comfort. It is something I must know from the past.

Sometimes a nice lady, who says her name is Lori, also comes to see me and while I can no longer talk to her, she shares stories about things we once did together. I think we were once teachers who worked together in Atlanta. Although I no longer know what a teacher is nor what or where Atlanta is, she, too, has a pleasant voice that I enjoy listening to. She says we have been friends for more than 50 years and it is sometimes bewildering to me when she talks about our past adventures because I cannot comprehend what she is talking about, but I am grateful she cares enough about me to come regularly and spend time with me.

Other people come to see me, too. My son, Drew, and his family comes and spends time with me. This is exciting. Drew has been the center of my life since he was born, and I just know instinctively how much he has always meant to me. Drew has told me that visiting and seeing me in this condition is very painful for him. I know that. I told him to get on with his life and only come occasionally. Life should be lived to the fullest by the young.

I sometimes wonder why God has allowed me to suffer this terrible disease. I know that God did not have anything to do with it in reality, but He has been such a major part of my life, it is natural to ask the question. I know that Alzheimer's is caused by breakaway parts of amyloid proteins that collect and short circuit nerve endings in the brain, or by a dozen other causes like an injury or bad nutrition. So many causes, so much damage, so much time wasted, and so many good people suffering.

My life has become limited in so many ways. Two years ago, I could sit at my piano and play songs that I had played all my life. Now when I am taken into the living room of our condo, I see the piano but how it works is too complicated for me. Music has always been my favorite form of relaxation, but that, too, has been taken away from me. I miss having music in my life very much.

Sleep fills my days and nights. I have always been an active person but slowly my energy and physical coordination has fled. Even the smallest physical task is beyond me. The kind ladies who are with me each day put me to bed, get me out of bed, bathe me, dress me, and feed me. I would like to do that myself, but that is impossible. While I am awake, I watch and listen; there is much I do not understand, but their companionship is comforting to me. Sometimes my mind is filled with snapshots of the past. Lately, though, I feel the need to sleep more and more. Sleep, peaceful sleep, is a blessing now. My mind goes to rest and I escape the frustrations of living with this disease. Naps during the day, and in bed and asleep by early evening. This has become my routine.

How long will this disease last until I am finally free? No one knows for sure, but please know this—you are loved just as I know I am loved.

Susie Thortsen Wasdin
August 2025

CHAPTER ONE

SUSIE'S STORY: THE BEGINNING

"Here we were in a small Iowa town, surrounded by mountains of snow with below freezing temperatures, while people were in bathing suits cavorting on the beach! It didn't take much to make up our minds."

Susie Wasdin

I was born in 1949 in Spirit Lake, Iowa, a rustic resort town on the western shore of East Okoboji Lake. I had two siblings, an older brother named Vern and a sister, Sherilynn. My parents, Gordon and Polly Thorsten, were hard working middle class people and they taught us the value of hard work and high morals. My father was a postman and had a 22-mile route that he served six days a week in rain, heat, and snow. My mother, Polly, worked outside the home—something that was a bit unusual in the 1950s—but which became a model for me later in life. I guess you could say my early life was typical for families then. Our family life was centered around our home, church, school activities, and community affairs.

Spirit Lake was a small town of only 1200 fulltime residents who knew each other and who kept a close watch over the community. During the summer months, the population would swell as wealthier families who owned second homes in Spirit Lake would come to take advantage of the recreational activities the area offered. Although they were seasonal residents, they came back year after year and blended into the local population. I had many friends among the youngsters in this group and shared many of their adventures. Boating, I recall, was one of the favorite things we enjoyed and East Okoboji Lake offered plenty of opportunities for outings, skiing, and picnics. Many of the friendships I made during these early years have remained over the years and I appreciate them very much.

Susie's school photograph in Spirit Lake, Iowa, 1958.
(Wasdin Family Album)

One of my dearest friends is Vani Ahlers. She and I met in kindergarten in Spirit Lake and our friendship has endured for more than seventy years. I remember she and I took tap dancing lessons when we were six years old. A couple of years later, she and I appeared in a talent contest on the Captain 11 television show, which originated in Sioux Falls, South Dakota. Dressed as Dutch girls, we were so nervous that when the Captain, Dave Dedrick, told us we could watch ourselves dancing on the monitor, we just kept our heads down. Nevertheless, we won the first prize.

Susie and best friend, Vani Ahlers, take first prize in a television talent show hosted by Captain 11, Dave Dedrick, at KELO-TV in Sioux Falls, South Dakota. (Vani Ahlers)

Vani comes to see me when she comes to Florida. She lives in Laurens, Iowa, but spends alternating three months in Florida. She and I have had many adult adventures together and share a genuine love of "thrifting." We still share the same sense of belonging together as we did in Spirit Lake as children. Ours is, I think, the oldest friendship I have. Whenever she visited, it was if the years that had passed had evaporated and we were young girls together again.

Susie and lifelong friend, Vani Ahlers, celebrate their friendship over glasses of wine. (Vani Ahlers)

Sports were also a vital part of growing up in Spirit Lake. Water sports in the summer and winter sports like skiing and sledding. The hot summers and cold winters, often going below 20 degrees, made an ideal environment for all sorts of activities. School sports also were part of growing up in this small town. We youngsters participated in many of them and physical activity remained a part of my life until recently. Whatever I was doing, Vani was always by my side.

The school in Spirit Lake was small because a town of only 1200 residents does not allow for a large one. Classes were small but meant that each student received close attention from our teachers. The foundation they provided served us well in future years, and I sought to duplicate their efforts when I became a teacher. Teachers, I think, are the best role models for young people.

Life in a small town had a few drawbacks. Because we all knew each other and because we shared the same values, every adult became a surrogate parent. *In loco parentis*, I think, is the Latin term and it simply means that every adult kept their eyes on what you were doing. One of the other drawbacks was the fact that Spirit Lake in the 1950s was so small that most residential telephone lines were so-called party lines. That meant that several other homes were on the same line and it was necessary to place any call through a local operator. One of my friend's mother was the operator and it was hard to keep any conversation private. With so many adult eyes watching you and so many ears listening, it was difficult to keep any secrets or to get into trouble.

Church was also an important part of our life in Spirit Lake. We belonged to the Methodist Church. One of the church organizations that offered young people a chance to meet and interact was the Methodist Youth Fellowship. I served as the president of our MYF, which gave me my first lessons in leadership and motivating people. I think youthful life experiences are the building blocks for your adult life. Religion has always been an important part of my life, and

Grace Methodist Church, Suntree United Methodist Church, and Georgianna Methodist Church on Merritt Island remain important to me. Corky Calhoun and his wonderful staff at Georgianna Methodist make attendance an uplifting and rewarding experience. Throughout my adult life, I have relied on my early and continued religious experiences in raising a family, in teaching, and in day-to-day life. All in all, I think life in Spirit Lake was a positive thing. It certainly gave me a solid core of values and an appreciation for working hard to achieve my goals.

My life changed in the early 1960s. I remember our family had been snowed in for four or five days in January and the temperature was well into the 20s. One night as we were watching the CBS news and Walter Cronkite on our small black-and-white television, we were surprised to see news footage of a missile launch at Cape Canaveral. While that was exciting, the surprising thing was the footage that showed people playing on the beach in Cocoa Beach. My family and I were dumbfounded. On the beach? In January? Here we were in a small Iowa town, surrounded by mountains of snow with below freezing temperatures while people were in bathing suits cavorting on the beach! It didn't take much to make up our minds.

When summer came, our family decided to go to Cocoa Beach on vacation. We liked what we saw and decided to move from snowy Iowa to Merritt Island in sunny Florida. As a federal employee, my father could transfer to the Sunshine State with no problem and my mother could easily find work in the burgeoning space economy. Vern and I would attend public schools that were many times larger than the one we left behind in Spirit Lake. My sister, Sherilynn, was the eldest sibling and was out of high school and stayed behind to finish college. For an eighth grader, any move could and would be traumatic!

Of course, the critical question was, "How would I fit in?"

That question was soon answered. I enrolled in Edgewater Junior High School on Merritt Island in the ninth grade and immediately got involved in school activities and made friendships that would last a lifetime. My brother, Vern, who was a year older than me attended Cocoa High School where he was a star on the football team. I was prepared to join him there the next year and had already been accepted as a majorette but fate has a way of intervening. The space program, still in its infancy, was expanding rapidly and the population of Brevard County was growing by leaps and bounds. Many of the scientists and engineers working at the Cape were highly educated and they expected their children to receive the best education available. The Brevard County School Board met these expectations by building Cocoa Beach High School, a state-of-the-art school that would offer the best in teachers and facilities. Although I knew about the new school because some of my classmates at Edgewood would be going there, I was keen on going to Cocoa High School because the school marching band had a reputation as one of the best in the world and would be

Susie as a majorette at Edgewood Junior High School, 1963. (Wasdin Family Album)

15

going to New York to participate in the World's Fair activities, and as a majorette, I would be going, too. It seemed my immediate future was all set.

Imagine my surprise when my father announced that we were moving from Merritt Island to Cocoa Beach. Why? It seems that Vern's future was the key to Dad's decision to move. The new athletic staff at Cocoa Beach High School was busy recruiting players for their teams and Vern's performance at Cocoa High had caught their attention. They approached my father with the idea that if Vern would transfer to the new school, they would make him a star and get him a college scholarship. There was a catch to their offer, however, and that was that our family had to live in Cocoa Beach. After mulling over the offer, Dad made the decision that we would move.

I was heartbroken, but the decision to move to the beach was one of the better ones for me. Life in Brevard County marked an end to the memories of Spirit Lake with its freezing winters and roasting summers. The images my family had seen on that CBS news broadcast back in Iowa quickly became a part of our everyday lives. We were, if I can use a trite expression, living the dream!

Our move to Cocoa Beach in 1964 and my entering Cocoa Beach High School proved to be one of the most important events in my life. There were no established cliques, no restrictions on who held leadership positions or what a student could be. The opportunities to create new organizations and to be involved activities were boundless. As a member of the first class to complete the four-year schedule for graduating, I felt I and my fellow classmates were developing a school culture for those who came after us. It was an exhilarating time!

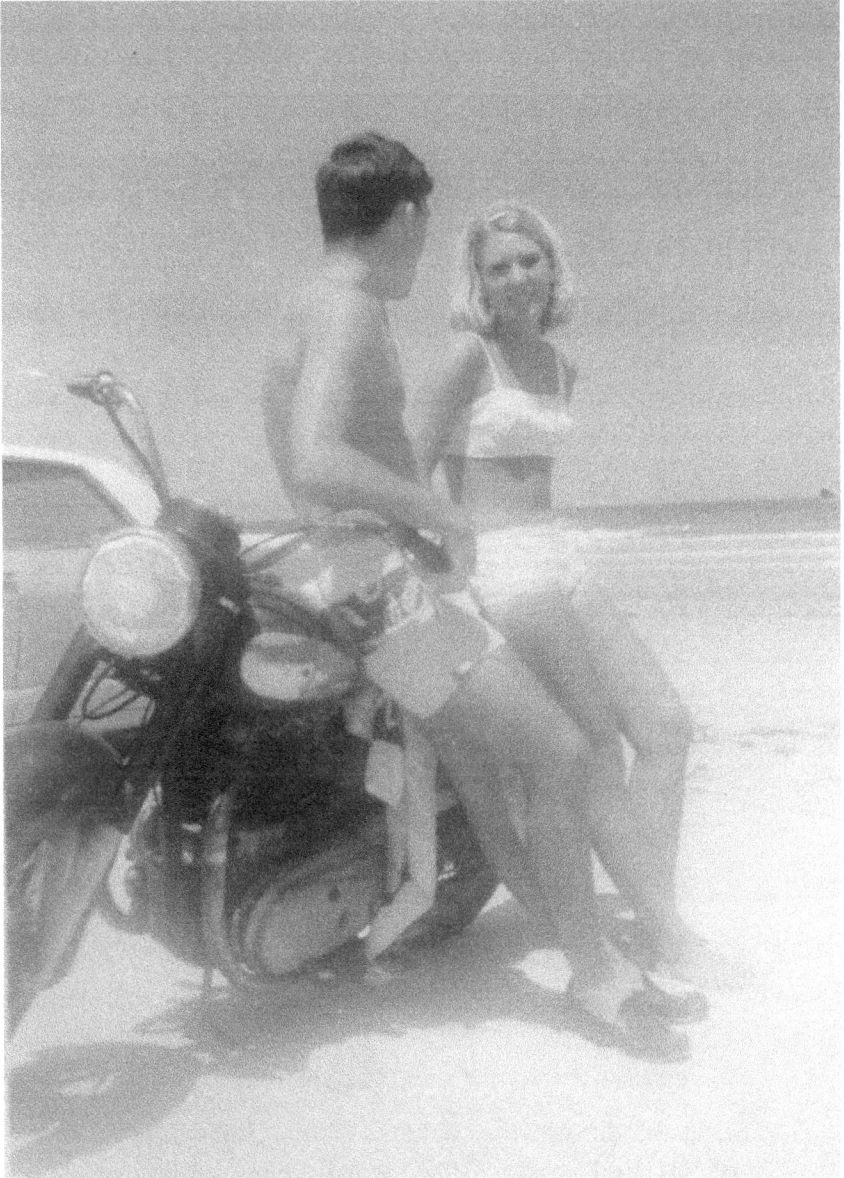

Susie and friend at Cocoa Beach, 1967. (Wasdin Family Album)

My dream of being a majorette and leading the marching band at Cocoa High School was met when I was selected as one of three majorettes at Cocoa Beach High School. I was also chosen to be a cheerleader for football and basketball games. We would hold our cheerleading practices in the gymnasium. It was a great opportunity to meet and talk with the players on the team. I enjoyed that but the grumpy basketball coach, Tom Wasdin, would accuse me of "holding court" and distracting his players. Neither of us knew what fate had in store for us!

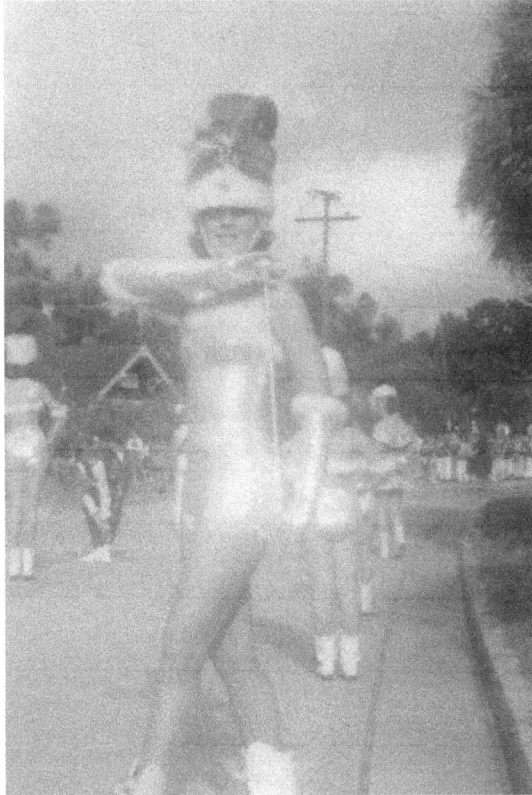

Susie Wasdin was the captain of majorettes at Cocoa Beach High School, 1967. (Wasdin Family Album)

I still remember our fight song after all these years—*March on you mighty Minutemen*—and we did! I loved being a part of the student body at CBHS. My best memory came in 1967 when I was elected Homecoming Queen, an honor that

I thought reflected my leadership and participation in school organizations. Looking back at the '67 *Heritage*, our school yearbook, I was given credit for having participated in sixteen different clubs and events, including student government, the debate club, chorus, and Beta Club. I'm surprised I had time to do anything else!

Susie Wasdin, all dressed up for the Junior-Senior Prom at Cocoa Beach High School, 1967. (Wasdin Family Album)

One of my most cherished memories during these years was my inclusion into the local debutante society and my presentation at the Debutante Ball. Although debutante balls were originally formed in England as a way to present young women who were eligible for marriage to society, the American versions have evolved into networking events that celebrate personal achievements, community involvement, and fundraising for charities. I still believe in those objectives.

Susie as a Valentine Princess,
Edgewood Junior High School, 1964.
(Wasdin Family Album)

I'll always remember the CBHS Class of 1967 and growing up on Cocoa Beach. They were special people growing up in a special place during a special time. I always enjoyed our class reunions when I got to see friends from high school and to reminisce about those great days at CBHS. Some friends are friends forever and some memories last a lifetime.

Susie Wasdin, senior class picture
at Cocoa Beach High School, 1967.
(Wasdin Family Album)

Graduation, however, opened the door to new opportunities and adventures and I was eager to get on with my life!

Life after high school was different. I, along with several of my classmates, attended Brevard Junior College (now Eastern Florida State College). I thought about pursuing a career in business but in the 1970s there were few women in business and fewer in business schools. It is hard to accept today but women could not get a credit card, buy a car or home, or even open a charge account at a department store then without a male to co-sign for her. Women have come a long way to where they are today. Still, we have a long way to go to achieve equality in wages and jobs. I made the decision that I would become a teacher. That was the generally accepted route for young women who entered college.

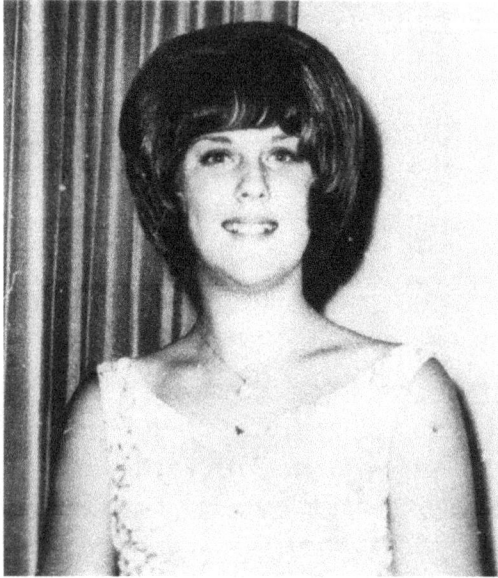

Susie Wasdin as a student at Brevard
Junior College. (Wasdin Family Album)

I remember an episode that happened while I was at BJC. I saw a brochure that advertised for students to go abroad and spend time working as governesses for European families. How different from my life in Florida. I applied and was accepted for a position as a nanny for a German family. I was excited! A whole different world was about to open for me. I got my passport, said goodbye to my family, and set off on my journey. The flight to Europe was routed through from Florida to the Bahamas, and after a short layover in Nassau, I was to board another plane and then be off to Stuttgart. In those days, boarding an airplane meant having to climb a portable staircase to reach the entry door. As I reached the top of the staircase and handed the stewardess my boarding pass, a nearby plane started its engines and the force of the hot air caused the staircase to suddenly move. It moved about three feet. I was already stepping aboard and fell through the gap between the stairs and the plane. I fell fifteen feet to the tarmac below, clawing desperately at the smooth side of the plane in a vain attempt to break my fall.

I was rushed to a hospital in hysterics. My fingernails were broken and I had an injury to my back, one that would continue to plague me for the rest of my life. A doctor gave me an injection in my fanny that put me to sleep. I awoke with blood all over the bed. The shot I received was hemorrhaging. When that was finally under control, the authorities transferred me to a hotel. Alone and without luggage or anything else, I waited until I was finally flown back home. My family had hired a lawyer who negotiated a settlement with the airline to cover the hospital and hotel expenses, his fees, and precious little else.

Back home, I took out a loan and transferred to the University of Florida in Gainesville where I completed my education. I managed to get through college by working several jobs, including managing the day-to-day office of a real estate appraisal firm. That was a valuable experience for what would come later in my life. Although college was inexpensive when compared to the cost today, living expenses were considerable for a woman from a middle class family. I also would travel weekends to Atlanta where I worked as a waitress in a restaurant in the Underground Atlanta entertainment complex. I envied my brother who had received a football scholarship from Georgia Tech and didn't have to worry about how to pay for his college education. The coaches at Cocoa Beach High School had lived up to their promise!

A youthful Susie Wasdin, date unknown. (Wasdin Family Album)

I did my student teaching in Gainesville. That was an introduction to the trials and tribulations a teacher experiences daily but it also made me aware of the rewards that come when a teacher has an impact on young lives. I remember I had fallen while riding my bicycle on campus and had injured my knee. It was very painful and I was wearing a bandage on it and my students were curious about what had happened. I explained to them that I had fallen and hurt myself. I will never forget one little girl who listened intently to my explanation and who then took something and hit my bandaged knee forcefully! Oh, the pain! I kept my cool, however, and didn't get angry. She was just being curious but I remember her as a sweet girl who never created problems. What an introduction to classroom trauma!

Armed with my new degree, I decided to accept a teaching position at Centerville Elementary in Gwinnett County,

Georgia, for three reasons. First, Vern was at Georgia Tech and having family nearby was important to me. Second, life in a big city after living in small towns had an exotic appeal. Even the small salary of $8,700 seemed like a fortune at the time but I had no real concept of how expensive living in Atlanta would be. I had a small apartment and three roommates. We were so poor that it was still difficult to meet the monthly rent, so we had to save where we could. That meant a lot of Ramen noodles for meals. My monthly salary was around three hundred dollars and out of that I had to pay rent, a car payment, part of my medical insurance, gas, and incidentals. I don't think I ever made more than $10,000 a year teaching. Third, Centerville Elementary was a new school and offered opportunities to grow professionally.

Susie Wasdin sharing a laugh with Tom
Wasdin, circa 1983. (Wasdin Family Album)

My friend Lori Mangiaracina still remembers my first day at Centerville Elementary. She recalls that at the initial teacher planning meeting, I showed up in high heels and a beautiful red polka dot outfit. As I made my way to join the group, I slipped on the newly waxed floors and fell on my butt. So much for a professional entrance. Things got better for me during the year, however, and I enjoyed my teaching days. As Lori tells it, "The first time I met Susie was at Centerville Elementary in Gwinnett, GA. It was a brand new school and this was our first teacher's meeting which was being held in the school cafeteria, with its newly polished floors. Susie walked into the cafeteria wearing her signature high heels, and proceeds to slip on the floor making her grand entrance on her butt! I knew immediately that we would be friends forever." Lori continued, "I cherish all the trips we've taken and the memories we've made whether they were at the wineries on Long Island, Chinatown in NYC, Sky Valley or Key West."

Lori Mangiaracina and Susie Wasdin pose together before the Titanic Runway Extravaganza Then & Now fashion fundraiser at Cocoa Village Playhouse. (Amanda Stratford, Florida Today Archives)

"Our 50+ years of friendship have been filled with joy and laughter. Susie has been the most generous, loyal and fun loving person I have ever met, with a work ethic beyond compare. I miss that Susie dearly."

One good thing to come out of this mishap was that Lori decided that such an entrance was an indication of a free spirit and she wanted to become friends. From that day forward, we have enjoyed our time together and for a young woman in a large, strange city, her friendship meant that I had a full social life. Young women, some married, some not, socializing and bound together by our shared teaching experience.

Because teachers had the summer months free, I was able to supplement my income by working fulltime at whatever jobs I could find. One summer, my friends and I painted my Volkswagen van with brightly colored flowers and headed to California. Once there, I took a job at a Howard Johnson's restaurant. One of the almost daily patrons was Pat Boone, the singer, actor, and American heartthrob. He was married to country music star Red Foley's daughter, Shirley, but he thought I was interesting enough to introduce me to his friends. He once arranged a date with Michael Reagan, the son of the then governor of California, Ronald Reagan. We had a single date after we discovered we had very little in common. It was nice, however, for Pat to do that for me.

Let me tell you how poor I was then. One of my roommates talked me into charging a new bathing suit on my account at Rich's Department Store. I think it was $6.00, a small sum really, but it took me four months to pay it off. I never charged another thing after that! Young people today think nothing of charging everything and not paying it off. I guess the work ethic I got from my family growing where watching every penny to make ends meet and paying your debts was ingrained in me. It's a rule I live by today.

I enjoyed teaching. Although my specialty was teaching English, I was also assigned classes in music, art, and physical education. Teachers were expected to cover the waterfront. We didn't have a break from the time we arrived on campus to the end of the day. We taught everything! I remember teaching kids in PE how to play baseball. Thank goodness for my athletic brother!

Being young and single in Atlanta during the 1970s was exciting. I met a lot of interesting young men and in 1976 I met and married Jerry Wendy, who was in the hospitality industry. We settled down as a young couple and on February 3, 1978, our son, Andrew, was born. Jerry took a job in Huntsville and we moved there, followed soon afterwards by a move to Satellite Beach. The nature of his work called for frequent moves, which I decided was not how I wanted to raise our son. Trust issues and ongoing conflicts in our personal life added weight to my decision, and, unfortunately, we were divorced in 1980.

Susie Wasdin with son, Drew, at age six months, 1978.
(Wasdin Family Album)

I returned to my parent's home in Indialantic, now a single mother with a small child and no job. I was concerned about how I was going to support myself and my son. One day while perusing the local newspaper, my mother spotted an advertisement for a sales person for a new condominium development, Harbor Woods. One of the developers was listed in the ad was Tom Wasdin, the former basketball and football coach at Cocoa Beach High School.

"You know Coach Wasdin," my mother said, "Go see him. Maybe he can give you a job."

That was good advice. So dressed in a dress that was too large because of my recent pregnancy, I went to see Coach Wasdin at his office and talked to him about working as a salesperson. I was nervous but felt confident that I could handle any job he gave me. During my student days at the University of Florida, I worked as an office manager for a real estate appraisal company, and my observations of agents in the office led me to believe that what they were doing I could do better.

"Let's see what you can do," he said as he handed me several brochures.

I had no experience in real estate nor did I have a real estate license then, although I later got one. The rules governing who could sell condos were somewhat vague, but as an officer of the corporation that built the condos, an in-house salesperson, I could sell with no restrictions. To meet the requirements of the law, he gave me the temporary title of vice-president for marketing. It was a challenge, but over two days, I sold one hundred units. Coach Wasdin was so impressed that he hired me as the permanent vice-president of marketing, which meant I was a fulltime salesperson.

That was the beginning of a new phase of my life.

CHAPTER TWO

TOM'S STORY

It seemed that whenever I gathered my basketball team together for practice, she would be in the gymnasium with a coterie of admirers, which was a distraction for the young players. I'd make growling noises and the group would disperse.

Tom Wasdin

I'm **Tom Wasdin and I am Susie's husband. I was born** near Waldo, Florida, a small town with a population of about 800 people. Peter Kerasotis has done an excellent job in detailing my life story in his book, *Once a Coach, Always a Coach,* so I won't spend much time on my early life except to highlight some of the basic principles I learned which we shared during our forty-year marriage; principles that we continue to share and which have constituted the bedrock of our relationship.

First, I am fourteen years older than Susie, and those years between our ages meant that we had different experiences growing up. Where she grew up in a small town with modern utilities, I was raised on a Depression-era farm with only the most basic accommodations—an outdoor privy, kerosene lamps, wood fueled stove, and no electricity. Ours was a chicken farm and chores came before everything else except school. Although we moved to a house near the highway when

I was eleven and we were able to get some of the amenities of urban living, daily life still centered on farm chores. Sports and other social activities were secondary to farm labor, a sometimes difficult thing for a young man to accept, but one that left me with the understanding that hard work was the basis for success and that nothing in life would be handed to me on a platter.

Second, Susie and I have always appreciated the principle that "family" constituted a core value for our lives. Susie enjoyed a traditional and stable family life consisting of her father, mother, brother Vern and sister, Sherrilynn. My situation was different. My mother died when I was only a few months old and my father, unable to care for me and my older sister, Dorothy, placed us in the care of his sister and her husband, Wilbert and Estelle Gunter. My father stayed on his farm but kept a close watch over us. Uncle Wilbert and Auntie Estelle—Uncle and Auntie—took responsibility for our upbringing and, because they had no children of their own, embraced us as their own. My father, who was still a young man, eventually remarried, but Dorothy and I remained with Uncle and Auntie. Their love and attention provided us with the grounding that we needed for a stable life. In reality, they were our parents, and they demanded the same behavior from us as any traditional family. They showered us with love but they also were quick to administer any necessary discipline. Susie and I applied these concepts during our marriage as we sought to incorporate a "blended" family into a unified whole. Birthdays, holidays, and special events has meant bringing everyone together to celebrate as a family. Family also meant sharing the ups-and-downs of everyday life. We celebrate successes as a family and empathize with family members at failures. Family is the bedrock of our marriage.

Ardent members of the Baptist church, Uncle and Auntie instilled a sense of appreciation for living by a strict moral code in all of our dealings. Susie has always shared her commitment to religion with me and our children. During our life together, we have enjoyed being members of Georgianna Methodist Church on Merritt Island, Grace Methodist Church, and Suntree Methodist Church.

Growing up on a farm meant that money was often scarce. I often remark that we were poor but we didn't know it. Money earned was saved for essentials or to pay for non-budgetary social activities. Clothes were patched and mended but always washed, starched, and ironed. Thrift was necessary growing up and the ideas of weighing spending decisions carefully has remained. One does not spend money that one does not have on frivolous things.

Susie Wasdin shopping in Cocoa Village.
(Malcolm Denemark, Florida Today Archives)

One of Susie's most endearing qualities has been her belief in thrifting as a day-to-day practice in life. Even as our financial resources grew in later life, she proved that she could dress stylishly by seeking out bargains in consignment or thrift stores. Credit cards are to be used judiciously and not as an invitation to spend wildly. While she had a more middle class upbringing than I did, she has always displayed an ability and an enjoyment for getting the "most bang for a buck." That is to say, it is not necessary to spend huge sums on items when simply learning what something is worth and paying only that amount is prudent.

I first met Susie when I was accepted for a coaching position at Cocoa Beach High School in 1964, a facility that had been built with the latest, most up-to-date amenities of any school in Brevard County. I had entered teaching and coaching when I graduated from the University of Florida and was employed by Duval County's Paxon Junior High School. I later became the basketball coach and physical education teacher at Paxon High School. When Cocoa Beach High School opened in 1964, it offered the highest salaries for teachers in the entire state. The offer was too good to pass up. My wife at the time, Glenda, and I had both been working and the new salary was more than our previously combined income. It was an ideal situation for us.

Susie was among the student transfers from other area schools to the entirely new high school. Her family lived on Merritt Island at the time, but her brother, Vern, was an outstanding athlete at Cocoa High School, which was where Merritt Island students went. Seeking to build a winning sports program at CBHS, the coaching staff persuaded his parents to move to Cocoa Beach where he would become a multi-sport player for the new school. The move to the beach meant that Susie would also transfer from Edgewood Junior High School to become a member of the sophomore class at CBHS. At Edgewood, she had been a student leader—a majorette, a Valentine princess, an officer or member of various groups—and once she arrived at CBHS, she quickly assumed a similar role there. She was a majorette, a cheerleader, an officer in student government, a member of choral and musical groups, and a member of a dozen or so other minor organizations. Her natural beauty and vivacious personality attracted many admirers and friends, which is what brought her to my attention.

It seemed that whenever I gathered my basketball team together for practice, she would be in the gymnasium with a coterie of admirers, which was a distraction for the young players. I'd make growling noises and the group would disperse. I'd always see her around campus involved in some organization or activities. We once counted the number of groups she participated in and we arrived at a total of sixteen different ones. She was the CBHS dynamo.

I left Cocoa Beach High School in 1966, a year before Susie graduated and before the year she was elected Homecoming Queen. I was offered a position as assistant basketball coach at Jacksonville University under my longtime friend, Joe Williams. Moving from Cocoa Beach High School to Jacksonville University was not an easy decision to make. During my years in Brevard County, I had made friends with a number of local businessmen, including Richard Stottler and Charles Mohle, who offered me a one-third interest in the ownership of the Cocoa Beach Pier if I could bring it out of debt. I accepted his offer and set about revamping the Pier and expanding its offerings. I was also able to hire several excellent individuals to help me implement my vision of how to make the Pier a financial success, and my connection to the Pier meant that I had a permanent connection to Brevard County—one that would pay off financially in the years to come. Although my job as coach at Jacksonville University would keep me away from Brevard County for parts of the year, I returned each summer to oversee the Pier operations and to coach and play in American Athletic Union sports.

Still, the allure of coaching and recruiting for a university was too strong to ignore. After considering the offer and discussing it with my wife, Glenda, a native of Jacksonville, I decided to accept the job. Coaching at JU was exciting and successful. After my friend, Joe Williams, and I had managed to take the team to the NCAA Final in 1970, he left JU to accept the head basketball job at Furman University, a bigger program and wealthier school. With Joe gone, I was offered the job as head coach, which I accepted. For three years, the program managed to achieve a remarkable 63-18 record under my leadership. Three successful years that included two trips to the NCAA tournament and a bid to play in the National Invitational Tournament, however, were not enough to satisfy the demands of JU fans who wanted to see the university again play for a national title. Increasing pressure to become a national champion, the lack of adequate funds to compete with larger and richer schools, and a troubled marriage ended my college basketball coaching career. Glenda and I decided to end our marriage, although we remained friends, and I returned to Brevard County to take personal charge of the Pier operations. My children, Steve and Lori, would visit me each year in Cocoa Beach, and we maintained a close relationship.

My relationship with Rick Stottler remained strong and when I asked him to give me more projects to oversee, he put me in charge of managing and selling a 45-unit condominium development, Chateau-by-the-Sea, adjacent to the Pier, which was convenient and which allowed me to work closely with Robin Turner, whom I had hired as the new manager of the Pier. Robin's management and promotional skills were superb and soon we had made the Pier into a "go-to" destination for locals and tourists alike. With that operation on a solid and profitable footing, I could give the majority of my attention to the condominium project.

To assist me with marketing units at the Chateau project, I hired a young lady, Millie Aleguas, as my Vice President for Marketing. We became an excellent team in completing and selling these units. It was during this time that I also learned four basic principles that became the foundation of my later business enterprises.

First, know your competition. To determine what our competition in the condominium market had to offer, Millie and I would pose as a married couple interested in purchasing a vacation home. We'd tour the units, listen carefully to the sales pitch, ask questions about financing, and then take that information back to our offices and adapt it to fit our project. Our goal was to offer more at a competitive price.

Second, work with regulators to reach a compromise. As with any construction project, the Chateau-by-the-Sea sometimes encountered problems that ran counter to the stipulations of local building regulations. I quickly learned that solutions came faster by working with inspectors to solve any problems than by butting heads with a confrontational attitude. By seeking a compromise, the inspectors were more willing to help find a solution, thereby saving me time and money. Compromise meant they could feel good about fulfilling their job requirements, while I could continue to do my job successfully. This approach also meant that you'd made a friend instead of an enemy.

Third, there is much value in joining various civic and advisory groups. During this time, I was appointed to serve on the Brevard Tourist Development Council because of my connection with the Pier. This group was charged with promoting Brevard County's booming tourist trade and with advocating for and allocating funds collected by a tourist tax. The Council was made up of local business people, hoteliers, and civic leaders who were motivated to expand the tourist market. It was also an excellent way to connect and interact with individuals in the local business community. These connections would eventually pay off by creating new business opportunities for the future. Although I am now retired, I still maintain connections with the TDC and other organizations.

Four, be ready to adapt your project to fit prevailing economic conditions. The Chateau-by-the-Sea project was a success, but one hampered by the Arab oil embargo of 1973. The resulting economic turndown wiped out the buyer's market after we'd sold one-half of our units, but we quickly decided to turn the remaining units into furnished and unfurnished rentals. The income generated allowed us to meet operating expenses until the economy recovered.

Rick Stottler was impressed, and, at his urging, I decided to get my contractor's license. Once I had that, Rick began to use me to oversee construction operations for several of the firm's development projects. Gradually, I educated myself about how to create and build projects enough to assume more responsibility and to become a part of Rick's firm, Stottler Stagg and Associates as Senior Vice President for Construction Management. My career in the development arena was blossoming. What was also a benefit was that I could satisfy my desire for athletic activities by playing on the Stottler Stagg softball team and the company's AAU basketball team. All the pieces of my life seemed to coalesce at once.

In the meantime, my relationship with Millie had been changing. From business associates to friends to lovers and finally to marriage. In 1975, we tied the knot. Gradually, however, the relationship began to fall apart and we divorced in 1980.

Thank goodness, the economy recovered from the recession brought on by the oil embargo and I was kept busy with new projects. In 1980, we started a new condominium development called Harbor Woods on Merritt island and advertised for sales personnel. Imagine my surprise when a stunning young lady named Susie Thortsen Wendy walked in and asked for a job. It was the beginning of a new phase of my life.

CHAPTER THREE

OUR STORY

I often joked with Susie that because of the fourteen year difference in our ages she would have the responsibility of caring for me in my old age. I was joking, but I pictured us growing old together. Susie, I imagined, would always be beside me as we began this new chapter in our lives.

Tom Wasdin

TOM: Imagine my surprise when Susie Thortsen arrived at my office at Stottler Stagg and Associates in 1980 and asked for a job. I remembered her as the Queen Bee of Cocoa Beach High School and the sister of one of the school's premier athletes but she was now a self-assured young lady that exuded confidence and certainty. I was impressed with how she had matured and how determined she was. I thought maybe she was just maybe exploring work options for the Summer before she went back to a teaching job in Atlanta. I wasn't sure that she could handle the job of selling condominium units at all but I decided to give her a try. So I gave her the temporary title of Vice President for marketing and sent her to sell new units at Harbor Woods. I was amazed. In two days, she sold 100 units. She was a natural; her good looks, sense of style, outgoing personality, and grasp of what did and did not appeal to buyers proved the right combination for selling.

41

What started as a test employment was immediately changed to a permanent position.

SUSIE: I don't think Tom realized how determined I was to change my life and to start a new career that, based on hard work and knowledge, would give me and my son, Drew, a better life. While I would certainly miss life in Atlanta, I had a built-in support system in Brevard County and I was determined to make the most of my new opportunity. I was also determined to learn the ins and outs of real estate development. As long as Tom was willing to teach me, I was determined to learn.

TOM: I don't think I have ever met anyone as eager to learn as Susie was. My old coaching instincts kicked in and I quickly shared my knowledge with her. She was bright, personable, and able to relate to potential customers. Eager to improve her financial condition, she quickly got her real estate license and expanded her sales activities. In the meantime, our personal relationship was strengthening. My divorce from Millie was final and her divorce from Jerry was also final. There were many social functions to attend and because we were two single people, we sort of decided to go together. What started as a friendship soon evolved into much more. Because we were co-workers, we kept much of our relationship secret at first but eventually people began to see us as a couple. By 1985, after five years in a relationship, we decided to get married. Over the years we became so close that we had no secrets from one another. So Susie was especially helpful and supportive during this period as my trigeminal neuralgia, which had become almost unbearable, worsened. Her unselfish support made me realize that she was special. It was to be my fourth marriage and her second one. I hoped that it would be my last one, and it has lasted forty years.

SUSIE: As a good daughter, what could I do but obey my mother who had looked at me one day and said, "This is the man for you, Susie. He's everything you could ever want in a husband." She was right! So, too, were our friends, Jeanne and Doc Kelley, who informed Tom that I was the one for him. Thanks, guys!

Susie and Doc Kelley at Tom's signing for *Once a Coach, Always a Coach*. (Jeanne Kelley, 2014)

Of course, Tom had teased me about getting married often during our relationship. So when we planned a weekend in Key West, I decided to take the bull by the horns. I didn't tell him what I had planned, but I had a wedding announcement printed up before hand and mailed it to our friends and family. Sometimes a girl has to do what a girl has to do!

Susie becomes Mrs. Tom Wasdin in
Key West, August 21, 1985

TOM: Susie was smart and sneaky. I couldn't back out because the announcements were already in the mail. The truth was that she forced my hand to take the final step in our relationship, and I have never regretted it. Who would have ever imagined that the grumpy basketball coach from Cocoa Beach High School and the beautiful cheerleader would wind up together?

Always up for a party, Susie seems to be enjoying her birthday, circa 1985. (Wasdin Family Album)

SUSIE: What was amazing to me during our early years together was how well Tom hid his constant TN pain from the world. He had developed mechanisms that allowed him to cope with the acute pain spasms until they passed. Although he tried to hide the pain from me at first, that was impossible as we grew closer. Together, we set out to find a cure—a difficult task because nobody knew anything about the disease or its cause. This eventually meant trips to various clinics in different cities to visit with different doctors who suggested different treatments to possibly end his suffering. Some treatments, such as Tegretol, provided some relief, but eventually even astronomical doses of this drug and others could not alleviate the cause of this disease nor do more than provide a few hours of no pain. The pain was so bad that Tom was taking four or five times the recommended dosage just to keep functioning. When he suffered, I suffered because there was nothing that I could do to help except to be by his side. Over the next ten years, Tom suffered physically and, perhaps just as much, emotionally when his beloved Auntie Estelle died in 1989. Yet through it all, he and I tried to maintain a normal family life.

He was determined to be the best father to Drew as possible, and he worked with him on his basketball training and in providing the most stable family life possible. He drew on his experiences as an absentee father for his children by Glenda—Lori and Steve—and on his years as a stepfather to Millie's two sons. I think his reward came when Drew, now fourteen years old, asked him to officially adopt him. In 1993, Drew's dream came true and Tom, with Drew's natural father's consent, filed the necessary papers. What had been a reality became an official one. Tom now had another son.

TOM: Being a full-time father to a growing boy was a responsibility that I cautiously accepted. Fortunately, I had my own experience growing up with Uncle Wilbert and Auntie Estelle, whose unselfish love as surrogate parents gave me a stable home environment, and I often relied on the lessons learned by what they had given me for inspiration and guidance. Drew was now my son and I was determined to be a good father!

SUSIE: I don't think Drew could have had a better father. Tom set the bar on parenting. He not only coached Drew and his friends in athletics but he also taught him the same moral code that he had gotten with Uncle and Auntie. As parents, we supported Drew in all his endeavors, and when he had a game we made sure we were there to support him. It's a tradition that we now pursue with our grandchildren. What was amazing was that Tom was still suffering the devastating effects of TN, yet he never faltered. I tried to take as much off his shoulders as I could business wise, but I couldn't take it all.

TOM: Susie is being modest. There was a lot she could do and she did. The year we got married, we formed the Wasdin Group, our own residential construction firm. We set out to build houses in the newly developing Suntree area of Brevard. Susie had been selling homes built by the developer, Fairfield, and, although she was making a lot of money, she was unhappy with the overall designs of the homes.

SUSIE: The Fairfield homes were well built homes but they lacked the style that people wanted to make their homes unique. I would come home and complain to Tom about how I would have changed this design or added that feature to make them more sellable. He finally had enough of my carping and looked at me and said, "If you think you can do better, Susie, then do it." So I took up his challenge and the Wasdin Group eventually built 150 homes in Suntree. We lived in the neighborhood and our clients took great comfort in that. It was a hectic but exciting time for us. Steve, Tom's son, eventually joined the firm and took part of the burden off us. Tom's TN was getting worse but he managed to keep going. Very few people were even aware of his pain. As bad as it was for him, I think his illness brought us even closer together as a couple and as business partners.

TOM: Peter Kerasotis has covered the ins-and-outs of my battle with TN in his book *Once a Coach, Always a Coach*. Susie is right though; my illness certainly had a positive influence on our relationship and actually strengthened our marriage. It also gave Susie a chance to spread her wings business-wise and to become a reliable partner in our growing company. That's the good side; the bad side was and still is the side effects of the operations. The whole of my face is numb and I have to compensate for that.

SUSIE: Tom was remarkable during this time. Not only did he continue his relationship with Rick Stottler, but he continued to be active in our company. In addition, he maintained a full schedule of participating in various local civic groups and quasi-governmental organizations. His favorite, I think, was the Tourist Development Council, which promoted the creation of events to attract more visitors to the Space Coast and made recommendations for the allocation of funds collected from taxes on hotel stays. One of these projects resulted in the change of our telephone area code to the now familiar 3-2-1—the countdown for rocket launches. It was not all business, however, and we led an active social life as well. We found the time and energy to attend parties, to take family vacations, and to participate in exercise programs and to play sports. I think not many people know this, but he is an excellent dancer.

I learned from him the value of giving back to the community that had given so much to us. It was a principle that has dominated our life together. Even today, we still practice that and make giving—time, money, and talent— to worthwhile organizations a significant part of our annual budget.

TOM: I've always believed that a person's success in life is not due entirely to that person's efforts but also includes help and assistance from his or her business associates, members of the community, friends, and contacts made in the political, civic, and social arenas. A person cannot realistically claim to have "done it by myself." I often think of the expression it takes a village to raise a child and I know that to be successful in business takes not only individual effort but by taking advantage of the support and opportunities offered by others. I think once a person becomes successful in business, he or she has an obligation to repay those who helped along the way. Susie and I have shared this belief throughout our marriage and we have tried to show our gratitude by sharing our success by philanthropic contributions to worthwhile civic and charitable causes. I guess this is part of the glue that has held our marriage together for forty years. To acquire wealth is a worthy goal but that also brings with it an obligation to return a portion of your wealth to those that made success possible. To paraphrase an old southern proverb, "You dance with who brung ya." You stay loyal to those who helped and to the people who gave you your values.

SUSIE: Like Tom, I was raised with a strong moral code that stressed how we are all dependent upon others. While Tom was raised in a strongly Southern Baptist home as a youngster, I was raised in an equally strong Methodist home. The lessons taught were virtually the same—love God, family, your neighbors, and help where help is needed. That help needed might be financial, emotional, or just friendship. It doesn't matter; you help where help is needed.

Not only was Tom active in our business and in civic and philanthropic affairs, but he was also becoming well known in political circles. Local politicians sought him out for his advice and for contributions, while state and national politicians did also. The list of political figures who sought his support is long—Lawton Chiles, Jeb Bush, Rick Scott, Bill Posey, Charlie Crist, Steve Pajcic, several Brevard

County commissioners, and legislative candidates were among them. Although we were registered Democrats at the time, candidates from both parties sought him out. He was somewhat of a political guru who urged moderation and compassion. What this meant also was that a whole new realm of social activities opened up for us. We attended a lot of political events, including the 2001 inauguration of George W. Bush. Tom, you remember. That was when my mink coat caught fire because someone moved a candle and you had to take it outside and put it out in the snow. What a party!

Tom and Susie Wasdin with Jeb Bush, candidate for governor of Florida. (Wasdin Family Album, 1999)

In addition to his involvement in politics, Tom was also receiving recognition for his achievements as Jacksonville University's head basketball coach. Few people know this, but he is ranked eighth among all active basketball coaches from 1970-1973. He won an amazing 63 games while losing only 18. With that outstanding record behind him, few people in the world of sports could understand why he would walk away from active coaching. He could have gone on to bigger schools with more resources, but he felt every loss as a personal failing and fan pressure to win a national title took its toll. Still, he didn't walk far from coaching. As if he didn't have enough on his plate already with business and his disease, he remained actively involved in local AAU (American Athletic Union) programs and with serving as an unpaid advisor to the Brevard Community College basketball program. Dr. Maxwell King, the president of the college, sought his advice when selecting a head coach. Eventually Tom and I decided to bolster the college's athletic program by creating an endowed chair—the Wasdin Family Faculty Chair for Men's Basketball. Of course, that brought another round of social and sports events. Just keeping up with Tom was a full time job, but I loved it.

Tom and Susie Wasdin with Jeremy and Evie Shulman. Jeremy is one of the young coaches that Tom mentors. (Wasdin Family Album)

TOM: Susie can talk about how busy I was all she wants, but she kept a full schedule also. At one time, we sat down and listed the various charities, civic groups, and community organizations she was involved with as a fund raiser or leader and it came to an amazing nineteen. Was I busy? Yes, but so was she! Fundraisers, donor parties, and special events occupied a great deal of our time to say nothing of the parties and adventures we shared with friends. She was a veritable whirlwind of activity for groups she supported.

Susie Wasdin, who is co-chairing the Tuxes and Tails Gala with her husband Tom, stands with Theresa Clifton, Executive Director, Central Brevard Humane Society, and Buddy, a Jack Russell terrier. (Malcolm Denemark, Florida Today Archives)

SUSIE: Although Tom had been out of active coaching for many years, he maintained close ties with those who had played for him. One of the great pleasures for me was getting to meet most of these players and their families. Artis

Gilmore and his wife, Enola Gay, were frequent visitors, and, so, too, were Pembrook Burrows and his wife, Pilar. Tom always referred to them as part of his family and they, in turn, continue to turn to him for advice, emotional support, and occasionally financial help. It was heartwarming to see how much they valued him after all these years. It just goes to show how much of an impact he had on their lives. I must confess, however, that having two seven-foot-something men standing by your side can be a little intimidating, but they are such gentle souls!

Pembrook Burrows and his wife, Pilar, pose with Tom and Susie. Pembrook was a member of Jacksonville University's run for the NCAA championship in 1970. (Wasdin Family Album)

TOM: Susie welcomed my old players and their spouses into our lives. Although I'm sure she heard the same old stories over and over, she never complained. They were my friends, and like everything else, we shared them.

After we sold Kennedy Point condominiums and marina, we decided to go another way in business. Harrison P. Van Vanderslice, who died in in 2008, placed his multiple properties in Cocoa Village on the market before his death and we purchased them along with several others around 1999 or 2000. These included the historic apartment building at 630 Brevard Avenue built in the 1920s. Instead of constructing new projects, our company became a property management company, although I kept my general contractor's license until 2008. Today, we have around one hundred and fifty different properties—condo units, Vrbo units, apartment buildings and other properties. We changed our company name to Wasdin Properties and hired a full staff to do the necessary maintenance, marketing, and record keeping. Susie adapted to the new operation very fast and she assumed responsibility for collecting the rent on them. I found it amusing when she changed her email address to "rentlady1," just to let our tenants know she was in charge. Her humor certainly aided her in fulfilling her new job.

SUSIE: Getting out of the residential construction game and concentrating more on property management gave Tom and me the time we wanted to travel and enjoy our time together. It also allowed us to purchase a seasonal vacation home in Sky Valley, Georgia. This was what we had been working so hard for—time and enough financial resources to travel and enjoy life. We have visited and played some of the world's best golf courses like Doral, Sawgrass, St. Andrews and Carnoustie in Scotland, but there are other things that are out there waiting for us—Alaska, the Panama Canal, maybe a Viking cruise on the great rivers of Europe. Tom was an excellent golfer, although he has had to give that up. We were fully prepared to live out retirement doing whatever we wanted.

Susie and Tom Wasdin relax at their condominium in Sky Valley, Georgia. (Wasdin Family Album)

Susie Wasdin posing on the golf course overlook at the Wasdin's condomium in Sky Valley, Georgia. (Wasdin Family Album)

TOM: I often joked with Susie that because of the fourteen year difference in our ages she would have the responsibility of caring for me in my old age. I was joking, but I pictured us growing old together. Susie, I imagined, would always be beside me as we began this new chapter in our lives. I could not have been more wrong!

CHAPTER FOUR

THE BEST LAID PLANS...TOM'S STORY CONTINUES

I knew something was happening with Susie, but I didn't know what.

Tom Wasdin

With our financial future assured, Susie and I looked forward to living the kind of retirement that would have seemed impossible in rural Waldo, Florida and small town Spirit Lake, Iowa. Planning our happy retirement meant taking care of all the end-of-life necessities so that our family members would be relieved of that responsibility. Our wills were drawn up, our financial resources allocated, and our business largely managed by professionals. We made sure that our children and grandchildren were informed about what they would be receiving on our deaths and that those funds were in place for distribution. Sadly, I had learned that lesson when my father died and I received only a portion of what I had been led to believe I would receive. Taking care of family has been and remains an important rule by which we live and by ensuring that each family member knows what he or she gets and that their inheritance is safe and waiting for them eliminates any ill will or infighting.

Everything in our lives seemed set, but as the old Scottish

poem goes, "The best laid plans of mice and men often go astray" and so it was in our lives. Our plans of traveling, skiing, and golfing our way through what was supposed to be the golden years began to unravel around 2018 when Susie, who had a nearly photographic memory for people, would quietly ask me who someone was when we attended public events. What was disturbing was that usually it was someone she had known for years. We dismissed this as the memory loss that happens as one ages, and we sought to bolster our memory with over-the-counter aids like Prevagen, a popular dietary supplement that relies on the synthesized ingredient, apoaequorin. It didn't help Susie, and her memory continued to decline, although it was gradual.

Lindsay Wasdin, Lori Mangiaracina, and Susie Wasdin at a Brevard County fundraiser. (Wasdin Family Album)

By 2021, Susie was displaying more of the attributes of Alzheimer's, such as becoming irritated over minor things at work and becoming less social. Social events were still important to her, but they became carefully planned ones. She enjoyed dressing up and participating in them. While her memory slowly faded, Susie remained the beautiful and stylish woman that I fell in love with. Checkups with her doctors pronounced her as healthy and physically fit, but she knew that something was changing and it was frustrating for the active woman she had been to not be in control. Slowly realizing that her memory loss was getting worse, she withdrew from the organizations she had always supported. One of the most devastating to her, I think, was when she informed Stacy Hawkins, the director of the Cocoa Village Playhouse, that she was resigning from the Board of Directors. The Playhouse had been a favorite cause of hers and she had donated large sums of money to it, sponsored several fundraising events, and offered her advice on play selections. It was heartbreaking for me to see her give up this major part of her life.

People often refer to Alzheimer's as the long goodbye and that's true. Susie's decline was slow but steady. She developed coping mechanisms—most dementia and Alzheimer's patients do—that compensated for her decline but I noticed a slowly increasing lack of spontaneous conversations and a decreasing lack of physical activity. By 2022, she became more of an observer instead of a participant in conversations; listening instead of speaking, smiling to show her agreement, and nodding as if she fully understood everything. I have always thought that Susie had a most distinctive and pleasant voice, and it was heartbreaking to see her verbal withdrawal. She also stopped her routine of working out each day and became more and more inactive. Slowly fading also was her ability to make quick responses and small jokes. Most people could not detect the decline at first but I could. What I began to see was a mere shell of the woman I had lived with, loved mightily, and played with for forty years. My Susie was leaving me and I was frustrated that there was little I could do to keep her with me.

One of the things that I witnessed was when Susie, who often played the piano to relax and for pleasure, could no longer remember how to do so because she couldn't remember the notes. I offered to get her the sheet music but she turned to me almost in tears and said, "Thank you, but I just play by ear." Not only was this horrible disease robbing me of the pleasure of her company, but it was also robbing her of the small pleasures that made her life complete.

Over the next two years, Susie became less and less mobile and unable to take care of herself. This once fiercely independent woman was gradually becoming dependent on others for doing the simplest of tasks. I knew that I could not cope with her physical needs alone and I began to interview health aides to help provide the care she needed. As her physical health deteriorated, the need grew for 24-hours-a-day care and I was simply not able to provide that care by myself. In 2024, I called a conference of family members and health aides to discuss Susie's continued decline, and after much discussion, we made the decision to enroll her in the home hospice program, a marvelous program that provides access to necessary physician's care and trained personnel capable of ensuring that she receives all the necessary help with personal hygiene, exercise, eating, and transportation. As Susie became more dependent on others, I added various pieces of equipment to assist the health workers. A bed lift, shower safety equipment, a wheel chair, and other things that allowed her to be moved safely and comfortably.

One of the best things to come out of entering the hospice program was finding Robin Ericson, the Healthcare Aides supervisor, who has adopted Susie as her own special project and makes sure that she is appropriately dressed, with her makeup done, and her jewelry in place before she goes out. When we go out, Robin is always there to handle her wheelchair. One of our favorite outings was Saturday and Sunday morning breakfasts at the Merritt Island Pancake House where all the waitresses know her and made a point of saying hello. Although Susie doesn't respond verbally, she acknowledged this kindness with smiles and nods. It seems like a mundane things but this scheduled outing had become a big part of her life. As I write this, however, I am sorry to report that she has entered the so-called "end stage" of Alzheimer's, which means that she is immobile and cannot leave her bed without assistance, is unable to speak, and is unable to perform even the most simple tasks for herself.

Another event she had enjoyed in the past is attending the Friday night happy hour at the home of our friends, John "Tank" and Rhetta Sherman. This convivial gathering of about fifteen to twenty friends was small enough and quiet enough that she didn't feel threatened or lost. Everyone there made sure to stop and talk to her, and, like the society doyenne she once was, she sat in her wheelchair and smiled graciously. For several years, we attended together but, sadly, her physical ability to attend gradually lessened as Alzheimer's continued to ravage her mind and body. Most nights, however, she is in bed and fast asleep by 8:30. Now she cannot attend even sporadically, but until the last eighteen months, it was one of her favorite outings.

Tom and Susie enjoying a moment at a friend's Fourth of July cocktail hour along the Indian River. (John Sherman, 2017)

So, too, have family gatherings been among her favorite things. Susie and I have always provided a place for family—kids, step kids, grandchildren, and spouses—to come together for holidays and birthdays, and now the simple pleasure of being surrounded by her family is denied her. They may gather but she doesn't have a clue who they are or her relationship to them. It was interesting to watch her face light up with a smile during these get togethers. How much she actually remembers I don't know but I do know that she loved children and was amused by their antics. Susie and I tried to attend every sporting event our grandchildren, Brayden and Samantha, participated in here in Brevard County. Susie, who was always involved in exercise programs, having once been a trainer for a gym in Atlanta and some sporting events, enjoyed these events. Today, I try to attend as many as I can, but without her by my side, it is just not the same.

Susie Wasdin takes her grandchildren, Brayden
and Samantha Wasdin, trick or treating on
Halloween, circa 2015. (Wasdin Family Album)

Susie and I graduated from the University of Florida
and have remained loyal 'Gators in our post-student days.
For many years, we would make the trip from Cocoa to
Gainesville for the Saturday football games. As our finances
improved over the years, we made significant contributions
to the University's sports and medical programs, and, as a
result, were frequently invited to share the President's suite
with other donors. Such occasions added the element of a
major social event to the games, and Susie reveled in meeting
and socializing with new people. Since her illness, however,
our attendance has been curtailed. Her love of the University
of Florida is so ingrained in her personality that even now
when she sees a UF decal, hat, or other symbol, it rates a
smile from her. Smiles, not words, have become her way of
showing some understanding of what is going on around her,
and I live for those smiles!

Susie Wasdin posing with "Albert the Alligator" prior to a
University of Florida football game. (Wasdin Family Album)

A word to caregivers. There is a negative impact when
dealing with people with dementia or Alzheimer's, and that
is the loneliness that happens when your loved one gradually
withdraws from your life. In our case, Susie and I were virtually
inseparable for forty years, and her increasing withdrawal
and lack of mobility means that I am left by myself to find
ways to fill the hours. Although I keep in close touch with my
business staff and although I have created a routine of daily
breakfast meetings with close friends, there are long, empty
hours during the day and evenings that leave me searching
for something of interest to do. Some of these empty hours
are filled with either live sporting events or watching sporting
events on television. One of the most important social events
for me is meeting with a small group of friends each weekday
morning for breakfast. This is a tradition that I have been part

of for more than fifteen years, and I still enjoy it. It is sad, however, to see my friends succumb to old age and suffer the ills that befall them. Still other hours are filled when friends are kind enough to invite me out for dinner or other happenings, and my friends, male and female, are thoughtful enough to include me in many of these, but, despite their good intentions, it is not the same as it was when my Susie was in her prime. I miss that very much.

Another word to caregivers. Although Susie has twenty-four-hours-a-day care from professionals, be prepared to suffer snide comments and disapproving stares from people who don't know the full story. I have learned that some people are willing to criticize every move the caregiver makes, especially individuals who have never faced the task of dealing with a loved one with Alzheimer's. While the patient is constantly getting further and further away from reality, their withdrawal should not create a prison for the caregiver. I try to spend at least an hour each evening just talking with Susie, and although I don't always get a positive response, I enjoy these nightly visits reliving memories of our life together. If she is having a good day, she smiles at me when I see her and her occasional quiet murmur of approval is reward enough. She might not respond always, but I know she listens. It's interesting to me that when we have these conversations, I don't see the shell of Susie but in my mind's eye, I see the beautiful woman, full of vim and vinegar, that I married in 1985. That is how I always picture her. My Susie, my partner, my friend, and my life!

I know this book is entitled *Susie's Story* but at the risk of sounding too maudlin, I think it could also be entitled *A Love Story*. Although I had three previous unsuccessful marriages, I learned a lot from them. They were, in many ways, learning experiences, and I tried to apply what I learned from my past failures to our marriage. As my beloved Auntie Estelle would remind me growing up in Waldo, "Sometimes you have to go through the bad to get to the good." That was certainly true in my case.

In many ways, I have been fortunate in dealing with Susie's illness. In my Alzheimer's support group, I have heard stories of others having to deal with loved ones who become belligerent or combative alone, while others have had to deal with patients who are prone to wandering off unless they are constantly watched. Susie has exhibited none of these traits. Her withdrawal has been gradual and peaceful but still our health care workers and I keep an around-the-clock watch just to make sure that everything goes well.

I have also been fortunate enough to afford to pay for her helpers, a cost of about $220,000 a year. I know that most people cannot afford to pay for such care, but God has blessed me this way. I urge anyone who has to deal with a similar situation to research the kinds of government programs that cannot provide financial or physical help. I know that the federal Social Security Insurance program considers early onset Alzheimer's to be a disability and provides financial support for patient care. Some Medicare insurance plans also cover this disease and provide equipment and medical coverage. The Veterans' Administration also has programs to provide services to veterans suffering from this disease. Local support groups can also provide guidance to families seeking assistance. Do NOT passively accept this disease when help is available. I have included information on several of these programs in the Appendices.

What the near future holds, I cannot say. I and the entire Wasdin family are thankful for the days we still have with

Susie, but the harsh reality is that while she is here, we are preparing for the time when she leaves us for good. That is not a pleasant prospect, but a real one. Her legacy to us will be a life of love, laughter, kindness, and service to God, her family, friends, and her community. Our loss will be irreplaceable.

CHAPTER FIVE

SUSIE, THE MOTHER HEN

As the children in her extended family had their own families, I always laughed because she didn't want to be Grandma, but rather Glamma.

Barbara Jenkins

Wasdin Family Portrait. Seated, Susie Wasdin. Standing, L-R, Steve Wasdin, Tom Wasdin, Lori Wasdin, Drew Wasdin, Lindsay Wasdin. (Wasdin Family Album)

"Susie was very much the Mother Hen," a friend of hers remarked recently. "She had her son, Drew, when she married Tom in 1985. Tom had two children, Steve and Lori, from his marriage to Glenda. She found a way to blend them all together. She also took care of her mother and father in their old age, as well as her brother, Vern, and his wife when they were sick." That is the common factor in all the memories of Susie—she was kind, caring, and determined that nobody was left out. Nobody, regardless!

Drew grew up with his mother following her divorce from Jerry Wendy. While Susie worked, he was in the care of his grandmother and grandfather, Polly and Gordon Thortsen. An independent soul, he was frequently in trouble with his mother, and friend Jeanne Kelley recalled, "Her number one priority was her son, Drew. His nickname was 'Trouble,' and it didn't matter what was happening, he came first." After Tom and Susie were married, he lived with them. "He and his mother would sometimes have disagreements," Tom recalled in an interview with author Peter Kerasotis. "When Drew was about ten, I'd come home from work and Susie would be crying because of things Drew was doing. I knew from my earlier experience that I couldn't be the main, or sole, disciplinarian. So the next time it happened, I called both Susie and Drew to me. I told Drew that the next time I came home and saw his mom crying I was going to give him a spanking he would take to his grave. Then I told Susie she was going to have to watch me spank Drew. Well, he didn't want that spanking and Susie didn't want to see him get spanked. After that, it never happened again. They took care of it themselves."

70

Once that hurdle was cleared, life with Susie and Tom settled down, so much so that when he was fourteen, Drew asked Tom to adopt him. Susie doted on Drew and Tom was always there to help any way he could. Because of Tom's coaching background, he spent many hours teaching Drew and his friends the fundamentals of basketball. Drew was a natural athlete and became even better by attending numerous summer camps. Susie and Tom attended almost all of his games—a tradition that continues today with Drew's children, Brayden and Samantha.

Drew Wasdin has fond memories of life with Susie and Tom. "Growing up with my mother was a marvelous experience. I was showered with love and always had her support and encouragement in any project I undertook. We clashed sometimes as all families do, but no matter what happened, I always knew I could count on her to love me wholeheartedly. She was such a fun-loving person and made every adventure feel like something shared just between the two of us. At times, it felt like she was more of a co-conspirator than just a mother. Mom shared her passion for cooking, and today I am a very good cook because of her."

"When Dad came into our lives after they married in 1985, the adventures continued. His deep knowledge of sports, combined with my growing interest in playing sport, particularly basketball, added a whole new dimension to my life. He was always eager to help me improve my skills and become better. Mother and Dad attended virtually every game I played even when I was away at The Bolles School in Jacksonville, FL, a highly regarded academic and athletic boarding school located two hours from home. Their commitment never wavered. Despite the distance, they made the trip for every athletic event. Bolles became a place where

I truly flourished, both academically and athletically, and it helped shape who I am today. Mom also shared her love for the University of Florida, and we attended many Gator games together over the years. That passion left a lasting impression on me, and I ultimately ended up attending the University of Florida, something I know made her incredibly proud. Today, I've passed that same love for the Gators on to my own family. Go Gators!"

"I was included when they went to college tournaments and national sporting events like the NCAA finals. With Dad's connections in the coaching world, he introduced me to many of his friends. I grew to love this man who made my mother so happy and treated me as if I were his own son. When I was fourteen, I asked him to formally adopt me, and he did with no conditions, no hesitation. For my mother, that was a deeply important moment. She always emphasized the importance of family, and that step solidified it in her eyes. Family relationships were always a priority for her. She made sure my stepbrother and stepsister felt welcome in our home and supported them generously in all their activities."

"In-laws were embraced as part of the family, and holidays became cherished times where our extended and blended family would come together to laugh, love, and make memories. When grandchildren came along, she made sure they were part of the festivities, too. When my own children, Brayden and Samantha, were born, she quickly adopted the role of doting grandmother. She poured her time and energy into them, dressing up for Halloween, throwing elaborate birthday parties, and cheering them on at their sporting events. Just like she had done for me, she showered them with love. And her love wasn't limited to just my kids, she extended it to all her grandchildren. Every visit became an adventure under her care. That, I believe, is the hallmark of Susie Thortsen Wasdin: undying love for family."

"My mom was born in Iowa, and she had always wanted to take me on a trip there. Although we never made that trip together, I used to joke with her and say, "Well, I know two people from Iowa, you, and my beautiful wife Lindsay, who was also born there. I guess the old saying, you marry a woman like your mother, somewhat came true. Laughs."

"As I watch this beautiful and loving woman succumb to the ravages of Alzheimer's, my heart aches. She gave so much to me and to our family and had so much more to give. We were robbed by this disease, and I resent that deeply. But even Alzheimer's cannot take away the memories I have of her. They are forever etched in my heart. No matter what happens, I will always remember Susie Wasdin, not just as my mother, but as the woman who filled my life with love, adventure, and the true meaning of family."

Although Susie and Tom were busy with business and with raising Drew, they did not forget Tom's children. Lori Wasdin, Tom's daughter, recalled her first meeting with Susie. "I first encountered Susie at the bus station, where my brother, Steve, and I were waiting for our father to pick us up from the Greyhound terminal. As I stepped off the bus, I caught my first glimpse of Susie, and she struck me as the most exotic creature I had ever seen. It was strange meeting my father's new wife," she said, "but her warmth, kindness, and friendliness were immediately apparent." That is a recurring theme when people are asked to describe Susie— warm, kind, friendly, and glamorous.

"It took some time," Lori continued. "However, over the years, she blossomed into a wonderful stepmother, but it was towards the end of her life that she truly became my 'mom.'

73

As Susie's Alzheimer's disease progressed, I found myself gradually assisting around the office and at home. The time I spent with her increased significantly, forging a bond that would have been unlikely without the circumstances we faced. In 2021, after the loss of my own mother, I asked Susie if I could start calling her 'mom.' She said she would like that, too, and thereafter we shared many important conversations from that day on with a new fondness for one another."

"We spent our days together, whether it was daily workouts with Susie, Dad, and me, running up the hill by their house, or exploring thrift stores, attending doctor's appointments, plays, fundraisers and other social events together. We delved into discussions about the progression of her illness, reflecting on life, love, and the essence of truly living."

"I was struck by how strong she was in facing this dread disease. Remarkably, Susie rarely indulged in self-pity; instead, she sought to make the most of the difficult news we faced regarding her condition. Through our conversations, I learned more about her than ever before, which solidified her place in my heart as my mother."

"Learning important things from Susie was not a recent thing," Lori fondly recalled. "Even in my high school years, I gained invaluable insights from Susie. I would occasionally assist at the Harbor Woods sales office, where she took the time to impart her wisdom about sales and the importance of hard work. I vividly recall her recounting the story of her early days as a new salesperson at Suntree, where she would arrive early, stay late, work weekends and work through her lunch hour to ensure that any prospects that came through while others were away would find her ready and eager to help. Such lessons in hard work and resilience became deeply ingrained in me, shaping my understanding of perseverance."

Lori's brother, Steve, shared his memories of life with Susie. "I first met Susie as a young teenager and it quickly became apparent that this high energy, vivacious woman would likely be my stepmother at some point. I had no immediate idea exactly what force had entered my father's life but, as anyone that has spent any time around Susie would attest, she is not for the faint of heart."

"In Susie, I discovered many things. First and foremost, I knew I had found an ally. As many teenage sons would acknowledge in honest introspection, their father is an intimidating figure. She humanized Dad in a way that few others could and I needed that at that stage of my young life. She promoted my silly jokes with his reluctant involvement, even the ones about the dietary need for roughage. She leaned into the uncomfortable in a way I had never experienced an adult. At times, she felt much more like a partner in crime than a stepmother. For this, I will always be grateful."

"Although when I started working for the Wasdin Group fresh out of college, Susie and I had a few disagreements—a case of two strong personalities—but once I left the company and was on my own, the conflicts ended and Susie and I bonded. I was glad for that."

"Most importantly, she made Dad happy. I distinctly remember Dad's look as he observed her entering a room filled with the most interesting of people, and yet, none were as interesting and enthralling as her. He had captured a rare gem and he knew it each time he observed her interacting across all walks of life. That is the beauty of Susie. She could be anybody to anyone without limitation."

Granddaughter Kelsey Azzam shared her memories of "Glamma" recently, "Some of my favorite memories with Grandma are simple but deeply meaningful. We shared many Black Fridays hunting for bargains at Goodwill and spent countless hours playing dress-up in her closet. On Thanksgiving, she always let me help make the squash casserole, mashed potatoes, and her special salad, making me feel part of the tradition. I loved going on trips to Sky Valley, where she'd always surprise us with the big stuffed bear from her closet. More than anything, Grandma had a special way of including us in everything she did. She made sure we felt important at her events, helping us dress up and doing our hair so we'd feel special and loved. She would proudly introduce us to all of her friends and colleagues, which made me feel so important as a kid."

Kelsey's fond memories were shared by another granddaughter, Staisha Bannerman, Steve's oldest daughter. "I was lucky to spend as much time as I did with my Grandma Susie, and that time left me with memories I'll never forget." She continued, "One of my earliest is of her in the bathroom, fixing her hair and putting on makeup—always elegant, always composed, always beautiful. She wasn't the type to bake cookies, but she had her own way of making our time together special. When we visited, all us grandkids would pile into the bed she made up for us just at the foot of hers. It was cozy and fun." For Staisha, one of Susie's outstanding virtues was a sense of humor. "Even when she dressed to the nines and looked absolutely fabulous (which was always), she kept her sense of humor. She carried a fart machine in her purse just to get a laugh out of people. That was her in a nutshell—graceful and glamorous, but always up for a laugh."

Bannerman recalls the outings they shared, "She took us thrift shopping and out to eat, and she always knew how to find the best deal. I remember riding in her convertible, proudly chanting, 'Auburn stinks, Bama stinks, Gooooo Gators!' just to make her smile—she loved the Gators with all her heart!" Fun times were not the only memories Staisha has, "Some of my most meaningful memories are of quiet moments I shared with just her. Once, we went around checking on her rental properties, and I saw firsthand how tough and determined she could be—especially when we stepped into one that had been left in complete disarray. On another occasion, we visited her father, Gordon, in an assisted care facility, and I witnessed a different kind of strength. Even though she had the means to hire help, she bathed and dressed him herself. That said everything about who she was: loving, hands-on, and never afraid to do the hard work."

Susie's concern for others had a lasting impact on her, "When I became an adult with my own children, our time together changed in the best way. On visits, after I put my children to sleep, we'd sit and talk while *Law & Order* played quietly in the background. I'm so grateful for those quieter moments, just the two of us—no makeup, no distractions— just her, relaxed and being herself. I'm thankful for every version of her I got to know. She gave me her time, her humor, and her love. I'm grateful not just to have known her, but to have really known her. She is one of a kind—and I miss her spirit every day."

Grandson Hunter Stroh recalled, "Before I married my wife, I introduced her to Susie and Tom before I even introduced her to my parents. I valued their judgement immensely. Emerson says the world belongs to those who see through its pretension, and indeed the world belongs to her. Susie saw what those around her could, and ought, to be. She held us to it too."

"Susie impressed upon me the importance of paying

attention to friends and frugality; indeed, she never found herself short of neither friends nor finances. Susie would take the time to hunt down the best deals in any store she entered despite being able to buy the store if she wanted. In friendship she was even wealthier! Highlights of my childhood are replete with parties hosted by Susie, the Thanksgivings visiting them were always my favorite time of the year. She made what must've been hundreds of us feel totally comfortable in their elegant home. To this day I cannot comprehend how she managed to seat so many of us with intentional decorations according to who was sitting where."

"I saw Susie the way an English peasant saw the regal queen Elizabeth. To my shock and utter horror, my wife decided to bring up a story where she pranked a friend with a fart machine while at a girl's camp. I thought Susie would find that inappropriate, but to my even greater shock Susie was nearly lying on the ground rolling with laughter! We got her a fart machine later. After that you had to be very careful where you sat lest you find yourself the victim of the world's finest dressed prankster!"

Many of the same themes dominate the recollections of granddaughter Christine Wasdin's memories. "Some of my earliest and fondest memories are from the holidays. After we stopped having Thanksgiving at my great aunt Dorothy's, Susie took over hosting and always did it with such style and grace. Her home was spotless. She would hand mop the floors on her hands and knees using paper towels. I now do the same thing in my own home and often think of her when I do."

"Susie was the definition of fabulous. Always dressed to the nines, she had an incredible wardrobe of high heels, fur coats, costume jewelry, and glamorous dresses. Multiple closets filled with hundreds of pieces, organized in boxes we loved to play in as kids. She was always perfectly put together but never extravagant in buying clothes. Nearly everything she wore was a thrift store treasure. She had a true talent for finding designer pieces and pulling them off like a movie star. Thrifting with her was a ritual long before it was trendy. I think part of the reason I'm so cautious about spending money is because of her. She taught us not to buy new cars or pay full price for designer anything."

"She had a big personality. Sharp, opinionated, and hilarious. She spoke her mind, and I loved that about her. She was a strong woman, and I always thought I wanted to be like that. She would tell us stories of her days living in Atlanta, teaching and having fun as a fabulous, independent young woman. She was my first example of a modern woman living boldly, and that left a big impression on me. I'd like to think her experiences inspired me to become one too."

"Her sense of humor was unmatched. Her fart jokes, complete with fart flubber in her purse and even a fart machine, made us laugh hysterically as kids and adults, even though my Papa Tom didn't find them quite as funny. That dynamic between them was comedy in itself."

"I remember as a kid thinking I loved my Papa and Glamma's love. They were true partners and her love and devotion to my Papa was always clear for me to see."

"I have so many vivid childhood memories. Riding in her convertible. Sleeping on the floor of her bedroom during visits. Her doing our hair. Taking us out to eat (which was a real treat as kids!). Her introducing me to *I Dream of Jeannie*, *Gilligan's Island*, and *I Love Lucy*."

"At my uncle's wedding, I remember sneaking alcohol with my sisters and getting completely trashed (we were underage). We would have been in big trouble, but Susie helped cover for us once she realized what was going on and got someone to drive us home to sleep it off. Looking back, that was such a cool grandma moment, and she never said a word about it afterward."

"As an adult, I especially cherish the quiet, special moments we had. Just the two of us, or sometimes with my dad or my sister Elizabeth, sharing a glass of wine in Sky Valley or in Florida, looking out over the water."

"What has been hardest is watching her fade in recent years. Since I've seen her post-COVID, she hasn't remembered me, and that breaks my heart every time. I feel deeply sad for her in the state she is in now.. Her decline happened quietly during COVID when we couldn't visit, and by the time we finally could, so much had changed."

"Still, I hold tightly to the memories. She was truly one of a kind. Beyond fabulous, funny, sharp, and unforgettable. I'm grateful to have known her and to carry pieces of her in who I am."

Grandson Steven Wasdin shared his memories of his grandmother, "I have a lot of memories with Grandma Susie but one of my earliest and most cherished ones is when she took me and my sisters out for ice cream in Sky Valley, Georgia during the summer. I must have been no older than four, but I remember how excited we all were, not just for the ice cream, but because we were with her. After eating, me and all of my sisters argued about who should get the cherry from Grandma's banana split she ordered, and she eventually gave it to me. I remember how excited and grateful I was that she gave me the best part of the banana split. She had a special way of making everything we did fun and with her bright personality always having a good time to be around her. I remember a lot of laughter and the way she made each of us feel loved. She would make something as ordinary as an ice cream stop feel like a grand celebration. That day stays with me, not just for the ice cream, but because it captures who she is at her core: joyful, generous, and full of love. It's a memory I carry with deep gratitude."

Elizabeth Wasdin, another granddaughter, shared her fond memories, "When I think of my Grandma Susie, I think of someone who was always full of life, laughter, and a little bit of mischief—in the best way. She had this incredible ability to make everyday moments feel magical, and being with her always felt like an adventure."

"One of my earliest memories was when I really wanted to try coffee, even though my parents were totally against it. One day, I was with Grandma Susie and told her about it— and with a little smile, she said, 'Well, I think we should try it.' I thought it was the coolest thing ever that she let me have coffee. Of course, I took one sip and immediately thought it was disgusting! But she just laughed with me, and I'll never forget how special it felt that she treated me like a grown-up, just for that moment."

"She also once taught me how to do a headstand. I had no idea she even *knew* how to do one, but she surprised me by flipping right into it. I thought it was the most amazing thing. Then she helped me try it and we laughed the whole time. It was such a simple thing, but I remember feeling so proud, and so connected to her."

"Another time, she let me try on one of her wigs. She thought it looked great on me and wanted to show everyone. Then, without hesitation, she gave it to me. I still have it to this day and it reminds me of her playfulness and how generous she always was."

"One especially meaningful memory is when she took my sister Kelsey and me to visit her dad, who also had Alzheimer's. It was heartbreaking to see him that way, but Grandma was so kind and tender with him. I remember how she gently advocated for him with the nurses when she noticed his clothes hadn't been changed. It showed me just how deeply she cared for others and just how fiercely loving and protective she could be."

"And of course, I'll never forget the time we all went Black Friday shopping together. It was still dark out when we lined up outside the store, and my sister and I were right there with her, laughing, talking, and enjoying the excitement. She ended up being interviewed for a newspaper article, which made it all the more memorable. It was chaotic and crowded, but it was one of the most fun mornings we ever had."

"These memories are just a few small glimpses into the beautiful soul that is my Grandma Susie. She made everything special. Even now, as Alzheimer's changes so much, those memories remind me of her spirit—joyful, bold, and full of love."

The legacy of Grandma Susie remains strong with members of her family, and they share an unbounding love of her. Perhaps that is the right legacy to have.

FAMILY ALBUM

Grandma and Grandpa Thortsen.
Vern Thortsen, 2½ years old;
Susie Thortsen, 14 months old.
(Thortsen Family Album)

Grandpa Thortsen and Susie, at 14
months. (Thortsen Family Album)

Susie and brother, Vern, with father, Gordon, in Spirit Lake, Iowa. (Thortsen Family Album)

Susie, Vern, and older sister, Sherrilynn, in Spirit Lake, Iowa. (Thortsen Family Album)

Susie, three years old, with brother, Vern, in
Spirit Lake, Iowa. (Thortsen Family Album)

Susie, Grandma Thortsen, and sister,
Sherrilynn. (Thortsen Family Album)

Tom and Susie… (Wasdin Family Album)

Susie stirring the pot to make sure that her guests at the annual
Superbowl party are fed. (Wasdin Family Album)

Susie Wasdin, Jim and Johnnie Swann at the 25th Annual Volunteer Recognition Awards at Eastern Florida State College. (Craig Bailey, Florida Today Archives)

Tony and Sara Macaulay pose with Susie Wasdin during the Arts in Brevard: A Celebration of Brevard Artists event on Jan. 9 at the law offices of Gray Robinson, P.A. on Nasa Boulevard in Melbourne. (Brian Curl, Florida Today Archives)

Tom and Susie Wasdin will be among the hosts of the Run for the Roses Kentucky Derby party Saturday, May 6 at the Porcher House in Cocoa Village. The event benefits the Cocoa Village Playhouse. (Florida Today Archives)

Susie and Tom Wasdin, and their grandson Brayden, enjoy a Christmas Eve open house at their Cocoa Village home. (Suzy Fleming Leonard, Florida Today Archives)

Ray Corriveau and Susie Wasdin at Eastern Florida State College for the 2019 Florida Today Volunteer Recognition Awards. (Craig Bailey, Florida Today Archives)

Susie Wasdin with her Aunt Sally, 2003.
(Wasdin Family Album)

89

Tom and Susie Wasdin celebrate a birthday with their grandchildren,
Brayden and Samantha Wasdin. (Wasdin Family Album)

Tom and Susie Wasdin enjoying a night out in a local restaurant.
(Wasdin Family Album)

Susie and son, Drew, pose together before a University
of Florida football game. (Wasdin Family Album)

Tom Wasdin in an informal photograph.
(Wasdin Family Album)

Tom and Susie in their Sky Valley kitchen. (Wasdin Family Album)

Susie, exploring the sights in the mountains of North Georgia.
(Wasdin Family Album)

CHAPTER SIX

HOW THE WORLD SEES SUSIE

Almost 60 years after meeting Susie, I can sum her up as not only beautiful and vibrant but committed to friends, community and her family. Fond memories of Susie will last forever.

Tom Weinberg

For many people in Florida, the name Susie Wasdin evokes an image of a stylish, beautiful woman at a social event or fundraiser. That is one side of Susie. For others, her name conjures up the picture of an energetic woman, busy with taking care of her job as a member of the staff of Wasdin Properties—a shrewd businesswoman who worked closely with Tom, her husband, to grow and preserve the family fortune. That, too, is one side of Susie. To still others, their vision of Susie is a down-to-earth woman who scoured thrift stores and consignment shops to find bargains in stylish clothes for her and Tom. That is another side of this remarkable woman. Finally, some people see her as the doting wife, mother, and grandmother whose love of family is always on display. Who is the real Susie Wasdin? All of these versions of Susie are spot on, but concentrating on only one of them would capture just one side of a multi-faceted personality. She is all of these.

While most people seldom or occasionally are pictured in

the newspapers attending or sponsoring fundraising events, a brief survey of the *Florida Today* photographic archives from 1999 until 2018 show fifty-seven different photographs of Susie and Tom attending various events. Photographs from the Wasdin Family album record hundreds more. The amount of money that they have raised or contributed to different organizations or educational institutions is in the millions of dollars; certainly, justifications enough to validate the perception of her (and Tom) as powerhouses in the area of philanthropy. As their friend, Tom Weinberg, said recently, "Susie was a consummate fundraiser for local causes—everything from homelessness to Humane Society to the Village theatre." So true!

In 2013, *Space Coast Daily* named Susie and Tom Central Florida Humanitarians. In 2002, Tom was named Citizen of the Year by *Florida Today*, and in 2013, Susie was named Volunteer of the Year by the same newspaper. The list of their involvement as partners in philanthropic endeavors is a long one: Civil Military Council Foundation, Honor America, KLD Kids, We Care 2, United Way of Brevard, Florida Tech, Cocoa Mainstreet, Sally's Friends, Eckerd Youth Foundation, Melbourne Alumna Scholarship Fund, Space Coast Marine Institute, Brevard Symphony Orchestra, Brevard Museum of History and Science, Crosswinds Youth Services, Brevard County FAMUAA, Health First Foundation, Brevard Neighborhood Development Coalition, Satellite Beach Cheerleaders, Susan G. Komen for the Cause, People to People, Brevard Walk of Fame, Rotary Club of Cocoa, Florida Today's Reaching Out Holiday Fund, The Haven, American Cancer Society, Extreme Cheer and Dance, Space Coast Early Intervention Center, Space Coast Sports Promotion, Canine Companions for Independence,

Eastern Florida State College, Brevard Rescue Mission and the Women's Center.

That Susie was a great businesswoman is evident by her involvement in the evolution of the family's company. From selling condos to designing and overseeing the construction of about 150 homes in the Suntree subdivision, she was involved daily in the family business. In a recent interview, Tom was effusive in his praise for her, "She was a dynamo. Whenever it was needed, she painted; she mixed concrete; she poured concrete; and she hammered nails. She would look at the architect's drawings and make changes—small changes that would improve the overall appeal of the home and make it more sellable. She would design floor plans and hold open houses, just about everything to sell the homes. She was particularly helpful because this was the period when my TN was at its worst. I don't know what I would have done without her help in running our company. And yet, she could go from the construction sites to a society event, perfectly dressed and coiffed, within a matter of hours." Her involvement in the family's business continued until her Alzheimer's made it impossible. "When we moved from construction to managing rental properties, she took charge of the collection of rents and proved to be as good at that as she was other things." Tom Weinberg echoed that statement, "Her email address 'Rentlady1' reflected her zeal in managing over 150 properties she and Tom owned. If they failed to pay rent, she could get them out as quickly as she got them in!"

Early on in their relationship, husband Tom was impressed by how well Susie managed money. "One Christmas," he said recently, "I surprised her with a gift of ten $100 bills and told her to buy whatever she wanted. Imagine my surprise when she came back with receipts for her purchases and gave me back $800. Boy, did that make me appreciate her." Tom was not the only one to appreciate Susie's thrifty ways. Vani Ahlers, her friend from elementary school in Spirit Lake, fondly recalls the routine she and Susie had when she came to visit, "One thing we always did when I came was to spend time going from thrift store to thrift store looking for bargains. Susie and I are both thrifters. All of Susie's formal collection came from a thrift store. Items were thrifted when she staged homes, Her home is filled with thrifted items. Susie is the 'Queen' of thrifting." Tom's opinion of her thrifting habits is much the same. "Susie's not cheap," he said, "just conservative. She's worked hard for the money and she's not going to throw it away on frivolous items."

Husband Tom provided a look at another side of Susie. "She was my guardian angel when I was suffering from TN. She took great care of me, empathized with me when the pain became unbearable, shouldered much of my work burden, and, most important, kept my illness a secret until I was ready to reveal it publicly."

Family members were not the only people who experienced the real Susie. "When it became known that I was writing this book about her," Tom told a friend recently, "a number of friends wanted to share their memories of Susie."

Mike Henry, who was an upperclassman at CBHS when Susie was a sophomore, recalled her as a quiet, but effective, leader in school activities. Mike, who had attended Eau Gallie Junior High School before transferring to Cocoa High School, was a member of the first CBHS basketball team coached by Tom Wasdin. His memories of life at CBHS remain fresh today.

"Perhaps the thing I remember most about Susie was her

96

desire to include all her classmates in student life regardless of their standing. At school dances, for example, if she saw someone standing alone, she would invite them to dance. She was having fun and she wanted to ensure that everyone else did, too. I remember her as a confident and ambitious student, perhaps a little driven to succeed because of her background. I remember her as a kind, direct, and pretty much of a sparkplug—always involved, but never overbearing. It was a new school and the opportunities to create new activities provided the perfect environment for someone with her leadership talents, and she excelled. From cheerleading to leading the band as a majorette to participating in various clubs, we could always count on Susie. At our school reunions, everybody remembers her and what she meant to Cocoa Beach High School."

"Classmates remember her as the kind of person who would pick up the fallen banner if leadership waned. She had good friends, of course, but she wouldn't hesitate to finish the task herself if need be."

"I also remember her relationship with her brother, Vern, whom she adored. I really appreciated that kind of strong bond between siblings. I envied her."

"Our friendship got stronger over the years, particularly after she married Coach Wasdin. When my wife and I visited Brevard County, Susie would always take her shopping at local stores and consignment shops. TJ Maxx was a favorite. I know Susie was frugal and I often marveled about how cost conscious she could be in her private life yet so generous when it came to funding charities and cultural organizations. I think it was because of her early upbringing that stressed frugality and social responsibility. That is the Susie I choose to remember. She was and is a remarkable woman."

Jeanne Kelley and her husband, Doc, were Tom Wasdin's neighbors at Chateau-by-the-Sea in the 1970s. Doc also worked for Tom as the manager of the Pier. They served as "judges" on Tom's dates during his bachelor days before he started dating Susie.

"In the mid-1970s, Tom had a column called 'The Coaches' Corner' in *The Surfside Sun*, a local Cocoa Beach newspaper. He came to interview Doc for the newspaper and we became good friends. He was somewhat of a mentor for several of the young coaches in the area. Later, we became neighbors at Chateau-by-the-Sea."

"Tom was a prominent bachelor in those days and we got to meet most of his dates, and there were quite a few. The first time we met Susie; we told him she was the one! She was the most attractive and vivacious of his dates, but that wasn't the thing that impressed us the most. Her number one priority was her son, Drew. His nickname was 'Trouble,' and it didn't matter what was happening, he came first. Her character was always on full display."

"All our memories of Susie are very personal. Tom and I share a birthday, so an early memory was the surprise party she planned for us at the Pier—that was so like her! We had so many fun times together—dinners, parties, trips, and football games. Tom and Susie are, as everyone knows, die hard 'Gators while we are serious Seminole fans. It was always peaceful between us until U-F played FSU."

"The thing about Susie that will always be there for me was her realness. People saw this glitter girl who organized fund raisers better than anyone else, but she would tell you in a heartbeat that she only shopped thrift stores and consignment shops for clothes and cleaned all their rentals herself. When we had parties at our house, she was the last one there and was busy doing the dishes! She made life fun for all of us, and she loved her people absolutely."

"My father was an Alzheimer's patient, like Susie, and was a very accomplished, in-charge person. There was always a bit of that strong will still there with him, and I know that there are always glimmers of the real person that surface now and then. The ability to compartmentalize those times and cherish them is my hope for Tom during the rest of this journey."

Don and Pam Rutledge: Don Rutledge met Tom at the University of Florida and Tom hired him as an assistant basketball coach, in charge of the Jacksonville University Junior Varsity team.

"I met Tom Wasdin at UF when we were both pursuing our master's degree and Tom hired me at JU to help him build a Championship team. I met Susie right after Tom married her and I knew at that time she and Tom would be great partners for each other! Susie is not only a great wife but a wonderful business partner in their real estate business. Pam and I have been with Tom and Susie many times and enjoyed each and every visit with them! Susie you are and have always been a wonderful and loving wife to Tom and a very special friend to Pam and me! May God bless you both!"

Mike Blake is the current mayor of Cocoa and a teacher at Cocoa High School.

"I first met Susie in 1981, along with Tom and his son, Steve. Since that time, I have met her on other occasions and at different events. I especially remember hosting a fundraising event for a person in distress where she made a large contribution from the Wasdin Family Foundation. I will never forget the joyful laughter and smile from the recipient and the genuine pleasure Susie took from helping a person in need. It was a special moment. I also remember the exuberance she displayed at our Mardi Gras Paws in the Park event. She was smiling and dancing and sharing the good time with others there also."

"My advice to Tom and to Susie's family is to always be patient, show love, and understanding. Act like every story they tell you is the first time you've heard the story. I would also urge them to make time for yourself and allocate time for your personal life. Above all, celebrate the good times and the joy that you shared with the person."

Nick Wynne is the Executive Director Emeritus of The Florida Historical Society, which is headquartered in the 1939 WPA-built Post Office Building in Cocoa Village. He is also a former college professor, a prolific author, and a diehard University of Georgia graduate.

"When I first came to Cocoa Village I was aware of Susie and Tom Wasdin And their impact on not-for-profits in Brevard County, But it was not until around 2015 that I knew both of them on a different level. Each morning a small group met for coffee at Cafe Unique, then a local bistro. Susie would occasionally accompany Tom to these gatherings. Some mornings she would bring her grandson, Brayden, with her. It was interesting to see this glamorous social figure dote on her grandson. It made me realize that there was more to her than public image. She was a typical grandmother, watching carefully over her grandchild. That impressed me."

"I was also impressed by the fact that she would offer pertinent comments on whatever was being discussed. She had a natural intelligence that could not be faked. She also had a marvelous sense of humor and frequently zeroed in on some member of our coffee klatch. To me, this was an indication of the real Susie, and I appreciated it. There was a lot more to Susie than most people recognized."

Tom Weinberg is a former Chair of the Canaveral Port Authority Board and is a successful realtor and real estate investor in Brevard County. He is a graduate of Florida State University and an ardent Seminole fan.

"I first met Susie when she was a Cocoa Beach High cheerleader and I was a mainland Cocoa High guy. There were a lot of mainland/beach parties where we crossed paths. Susie was always the prettiest girl in the crowd. I ran into her again when I was attending FSU and she was a Gator girl. The Brevard county kids would often be at the same social events - most of which were in Gainesville."

"I didn't see Susie for a number of years after college until a chance meeting in Jacksonville when she and Tom were at an event for Steve Pajcic, who was running for Governor. Circuit Judge Peter Webster and I had gone to the event because he and Steve were friends. Peter remarked afterwards what a remarkable woman Susie was. She always stands out in any crowd."

"Years later, I ran into Tom and Susie at a Disney Epcot event. We were outside and, of course, Susie was dressed to the nines and every bit as dazzling as the event."

"Decades passed, I returned to Brevard County and had the pleasure of spending time with Tom and Susie on many occasions. When I decided to run for commissioner at Port Canaveral, Susie and Tom hosted a phenomenal fundraiser at their condo in the Village. Four years later she co-hosted with Robi Roberts another event that people still talk about today. Wow, it was an extravaganza in true Susie fashion!"

"Susie was a consummate fundraiser for local causes—

everything from homelessness to Humane Society to the Village theatre. She was also a great multi-tasker. Her email address 'Rentlady1' reflected her zeal in managing over 150 properties she and Tom owned. If they failed to pay rent, she could get them out as quickly as she got them in!"

"Almost 60 years after meeting Susie, I can sum her up as not only beautiful and vibrant, but committed to friends, community and her family. Fond memories of Susie will last forever."

Vani Ahlers has been Susie's friend since they were in elementary school in Spirit Lake and was a seasonal visitor to the Wasdin home for many years. She splits her time between Laurens, Iowa, and Florida.

"Susie and I have been friends for over 70 years. When we were in grade school, we took tap dancing lessons. We were chosen to be in a dance contest on the Captain 11 kids' show, out of Sioux Falls, South Dakota. We were little Dutch girls and were excited to perform. Although we were able to watch ourselves on the TV as we were performing, we were too nervous and looked at the floor. What a fun surprise to find out that we won the contest. It is a memory that will live forever in my heart."

"My best friend moved to Florida in eighth grade. However, and I quote, 'Childhood friends: a bond forged in laughter, strengthened by time, and reunited by destiny.'"

"Thirty years later, as if a day never passed, we were reunited by destiny. For many years, I would go to Cocoa Village to visit Tom and Susie. Susie came to Iowa a few times. We attended our 40th class reunion in Spirit Lake. What fun and a great trip down memory lane."

"In Florida, I was given the opportunity to live the glamorous life. Tom and Susie went to so many events. I watched them receive many awards, for all their charitable work and contributions, for Brevard County."

"What a treat to go through Susie's closet of formal gowns. I was thrilled to pick a glamorous dress for each event. The two of us went on a cruise together. It was a gift from Susie. What fun to pick from her collection for the ship's formal events. We had our pictures taken and it is a keepsake I am thrilled to have."

"Susie and I are both thrifters. All of Susie's formal collection came from a thrift store. Items were thrifted when she staged homes, Her home is filled with thrifted items. Susie is the 'Queen' of thrifting."

"There was a time, in my life, I was uncertain of my future. It is because of Tom and Susie, I was able to get back on track with my life."

"There are no words to describe Susie Wasdin, that would do her justice. She gave, from her heart. Always willing to jump in, head first, in any fundraising. I always say, Tom and Susie Wasdin are the best of the best."

James Davis: James Davis and Tom Wasdin were part of a group of golfers that played regularly at Rockledge Country Club.

"I met Tom probably 20 years ago playing golf at the Rockledge Country Club. I don't really remember how Tom and I hit it off, but he started inviting me to parties/fundraisers at his home. That is how I met Susie and of course I hit it off with Susie, too."

"So I was invited to any social event at Tom and Susie's, and I invited them to my social events as well and they always showed up for them. In my many conversations with Susie the one funny story that really stood out to me was when she was a school teacher (either in the late 60's or early 70's) and she was in Jacksonville at the Florida-Georgia football game and somehow she talked the guy who ran the big cart that goes up and down the sidelines with the TV camera on it to let her ride on the big cart. So she said they kept putting her on TV because she was riding the big cart and she's just smoking, drinking and having a blast, while all her students' parents back home watching the game on TV were seeing their kid's teacher partying it up on live TV. LOL! That is a great story!"

"Susie did tell me that while she was a student at Cocoa Beach High School and Tom was a coach there at the same time, all the students thought Tom was mean. She never imagined that she would eventually marry Tom. Another funny Susie story."

Frank Casey: Frank Casey is a long-time friend of Tom Wasdin and when Tom married Susie in 1985, he immediately became friends with her.

"I was lucky enough to have met Coach Tom Wasdin in 1968 (yes…sixty-eight!) while he was in Illinois recruiting my pal, Rex Morgan, to come play basketball for Jacksonville University. Rex did go, changed the course of the basketball program there, I somehow got to come along, and have known and loved Coach Wasdin since that momentous 1968 introduction."

"So I have known Susie since she and Coach married in 1985. Susie is amazingly happy, positive, engaging, sweet, caring, intelligent and industrious to name just a few of her positive attributes. And she keeps Coach in line most of the time—which by itself is an amazing talent!"

"Way too many fun memories of Susie to share here…and some she would prefer I did not, I'm certain! But…."

"Her parties were the best! A Kentucky Derby party, with

a live horse out front, Fourth of July celebrations, and much more in the beautiful penthouse she and Coach share."

"Susie and Coach's attendance at both my son's and daughter's weddings, where Susie reunited with old friends, quickly made new ones, and brought her unique sense of joy and celebration uplifting both events."

"Her great sense of humor, some self-deprecating, was always on display. My favorite perhaps was at a celebratory dinner where she and Coach were being honored for something (I have attended several where they were being honored for something) and she asked me to speak to the assembled group. I did so and attempted to be humorous—since the evening was a bit too serious for some of us unaffiliated with whatever cause it was we were there celebrating—and I had some 'fun' at her expense telling less than flattering 'Susie jokes.' She loved it and thanked me after.'"

"After a round of golf with Coach in the Jacksonville area, I drove him to meet

Susie for their drive back to Cocoa. We found her loading their van outside a consignment shop where she had found too many 'bargain' dresses to pass up. Coach had to put his golf clubs in the back seat as there was no room for them in the back of the van after her consignment haul!"

"I could go on, but I won't. Suffice it to say that Susie Wasdin is a wonderful person who was dealt a terrible hand that none of us should ever have to deal with. Bless her and Coach."

Barbara and Tom Jenkins: Tom Jenkins is the former County Manager for Brevard County. Tom Wasdin mentored his son in basketball, along with Susie's and Tom's son, Drew Wasdin.

"My husband, former County Manager Tom Jenkins, and

I met Susie when we first came to Brevard in 1986 . Our friendship has lasted all these many years. We were neighbors in Suntree for a number of those years. Our children grew up together with Susie's son, Drew, who was a frequent guest at our house. Our connection ran deep."

"If I were to describe Susie, I would say she was simply fun to be around, and very energetic. She was always up for having a good time. And we laughed a lot together. She was generous with her time and was very giving. She was especially active in her community with her time and financial support of numerous community organizations."

"As the children in her extended family had their own families I always laughed because she didn't want to be Grandma but rather 'Glamma.' That was Susie."

"Susie was an active caregiver to her mother and father who both experienced dementia towards the end of their lives. She was also a great sister to her brother, Vern, whom she also looked out for throughout his later years."

"We miss the old Susie and think of her often."

Peter Kerasotis: Peter Kerasotis is an award winning sports author and is the author of *Once a Coach, Always a Coach,* the biography of Tom Wasdin. He is active in church affairs.

"I met Susie through Tom, and I immediately recognized someone who was a giver and doer, and a tireless hard worker. She took a lot of pride in being Tom's partner, and I do mean partner in every sense. There were times when instead of saying Tom and Susie it seemed more appropriate to say Susie and Tom. She could be a force, and her work ethic was indefatigable."

"My lasting impression of Susie is that she was not above anything. She'd dig a ditch if need be, and probably did. She liked high society and fashion, we all know and saw that, but when you were with her on a regular basis you would see her roll up her sleeves when needed and get in the trenches. Whatever it took to get the task down, Susie was up for it."

"I remember once, in my home office, when we were going over photos for Tom's book, Susie was on her hands and knees, spreading and organizing photos on the hardwood floor, dressed up as usual, but not giving it a second thought. I don't remember if my floor was dusty that day, but it would not have mattered to her."

"When I had speaking engagements at local Kingdom Halls of Jehovah's Witnesses, Susie was eager to come and she and Tom would come together. It was always nice to look out at the audience and see them sitting together, and they were together. They were a team. The Bible says that when a man and woman marry they become one flesh, meaning united, and that's what the two of them always were. They were like one person."

Marilyn Green: Marilyn Green is a local real estate agent with the Pastermack Real Estate on Merritt Island. She and her late husband, Ed, were prominent civic leaders in Cocoa Village, and Ed was a member of the Wasdin morning coffee klatch.

"I first met Susie at one of the Wasdin's famous Fourth of July parties. She was decked out to the nines—dressed in her red, white, and blue beaded floor length ball dress. So beautiful, confident, and full of life! Susie wore the highest heels I had ever seen. I remember her telling me she ranked her heels not by height, rather by her 1-hour, 2-hour, or 3-hour shoes. I don't think I would have lasted three minutes on those stilts! She was beautiful, confident, formidable, and intimidating. So full of life!"

"Over the years, as I really got to know the Wasdins, I became increasingly amazed by Susie's energy and remarkable service to our community. I'm proud to call her a friend and even more proud that she referred to me as her friend."

"These days, I find myself attempting to make some sense of the many 'whys' I've found myself pondering. A big one is trying to wrap my head around how this remarkable woman, Susie Wasdin, who has touched so many, could so rapidly disappear in front of us. I just don't get why someone as vital as Susie ends up a shadow of her former self. Susie Wasdin will long be remembered as a powerhouse; a force to be reckoned with. A true 'one of a kind' who led by example."

Henry Minneboo: Henry Minneboo is the retired Public Works Director for Brevard County and a former Board member of the Brevard Soil and Water Special District. The Minneboos are lifelong friends of the Wasdins.

"I have probably known Susie as one of the longest of her friends because she was in my first wedding in 1967 in Brevard county, she was very close to my wife and that was the beginning."

"Over the years we had many, many times when we got crazy, but always enjoyed ourselves. Many times we would go to the Gator games and let our hair down because she wasn't known by all but many."

"She talked me into many things, especially our being Mardi Gras King and Queen of Cocoa, and once she made me Mr. Conehead. Boy, that was exciting!"

"Although Susie had a lot of class, she knew my back ground growing up in Angel City and knew I would enjoy anything risqué. She had the best stories, but many of them I can't repeat."

"I could go on for days but it's probably best if I keep it short. Unfortunately I am at the beginning of what Tom is and has been going through with my wife. When the time comes I am sure Tom will be there to guide me."

"Susie's name alone will bring a smile to my face for as long as I'm here. Tom may be called 'Coach' and Susie 'The Queen' by many, but they have just been great friends and I know if I needed them, they would be there for me."

Rusty Fischer: Rusty Fischer is a well-known restauranteur, author, and businessman in Cape Canaveral. His Rusty's Seafood and Oyster Bar has been a favorite of locals and tourists for several decades.

"Looking back to Susie's high school days, I remember her walking into The Surf with John Casbon, collecting donations for Cocoa Beach High. What a cutie she was—so pleasant, yet demanding, always in the kindest way. She had a way of getting me to give her whatever she needed and usually more."

"As the years passed and she grew older, we became friends. I always enjoyed our conversations. She was a beautiful lady, inside and out. When she married Tom, they were 'The Couple' — such a great team. They really complemented each other. Susie later became an ambassador at the port, and I had the pleasure of seeing her more often at our monthly meetings. She was a true go-getter. Whatever she did, she poured her whole heart into it. She got things done."

"Susie inspired so many with her energy, warmth, and unwavering dedication. Whether she was lending a hand, leading a project, or simply sharing a kind word, she brings out the best in people. Susie, we are all better for knowing you."

Dick and Marcia Hynes: Dick and Marcia Hynes are

neighbors in Tom and Susie's condominium in Historic Cocoa Village.

"We first met Susie and Tom when we purchased our home at Riverside Landing where together we are the longest residing owners. That was over 20 years ago, and over that time we have seen all the community involvement and support that was a big part of 'Susie in Brevard.' She had 'Social Energy' that was as large as Tom's love of all things sports! We saw it on full display at Riverside Landing when she held Kentucky Derby parties to support local needs... she even had a live horse at the party! Things were always surprising and fun when Susie was involved!"

"Susie was known for her 'style,' which was 'spot on' for every occasion. It's difficult to see that energy bridled, but the memories linger on."

Pilar Burrows: Pembrook Burrows was part of the basketball team at Jacksonville University that played UCLA in the NCAA championship game in 1970. Pilar met Susie through her husband and became friends in 1990.

"I met Susie through my husband Pembrook Burrows III."

"I first met Susie in August 1990 at the Jacksonville University N.C.A.A. Finalist Reunion-1970. She made me feel comfortable as if we had known each other for years. We later attended several glamorous events she chaired for charity as only she could do. Susie was always dressed and looked like a billionaire, but Susie was so kind and down to earth that anyone could fit right in with her. Susie taught me her secret on how to look and ride in style like a billionaire, LOL."

"When Pembrook was the Masonic Illustrious Potentate in 2010, Susie and Tom attended the Ball. They were the only white people there. Susie fit right in with us doing the line dance called the Electric Slide. I think she did it better than the rest of us."

"Susie was definitely a giver from her heart and gave to so many people and charities. She was the fundraising Queen. Susie taught me how to do fundraisers. I tried what Susie taught me and it really worked. I raised a lot of money."

"If you were around Susie, you already knew it was going to be a good time and full of laughs. My, oh my, the stories I can tell of how Susie made me laugh."

"It broke my heart when I was calling, texting and emailing Susie and she was not responding. When I saw Susie at Coach Joe Williams' funeral, she looked at me differently, smiled, talked very little, but she wasn't the same Susie to me. I later found out why."

"I was so happy to see Susie at Tom's 89th birthday party. I asked her permission to take a picture with her and Susie just looked at me, smiled as to say it was ok. Susie is definitely my friend."

"I will never forget the Susie I knew before Alzheimer's, even though I love Susie just as much now as I did then, if not more."

"I'd sum up the old Susie this way: Loves Tom, my friend, best dressed billionaire, beautiful, loving, giving, kind, witty, down to earth, fundraising Queen."

Shirley Lanni: Shirley and her late husband, Captain Ed, have been civic and social icons in Historic Cocoa Village for many years.

"Susie has been a dear friend of mine for many years. She and I worked together on several fundraising projects, including raising money—some $30,000—for the Cocoa High School Stadium. We also worked together on the Kentucky Derby celebrations which raised money for Cocoa

111

Main Street. She and Tom invited my late husband, Captain Ed, and me to many parties at their condo along the riverfront. She was a vivacious, funny woman who made every project a fun time. She had an enormous portfolio of important people and she would dive into it to get the names and numbers of people who would contribute to whatever causes we were supporting."

"I miss seeing and enjoying Susie's company. The community has lost a dynamic and forceful civic leader and philanthropist. Alzheimer's is a terrible disease. I hope that a cure can be found one day. Go in peace and love, my friend."

Theresa Clifton: Theresa Clifton is the Executive Director of the Brevard Humane Society.

"I don't remember exactly when I met Susie, seems I just always knew her. She was that kind of person, once she got to know you, she would remember special details about you."

"For example, sometime in my 30s (I am now 66 years old), Susie took me and my sister, Connie, backstage at an Allman Brothers concert at the Cocoa Expo so we could meet Greg Allman. Susie knew I was a diehard Cher fan and Greg had once been married to Cher so it was a huge thrill for me—to say nothing of my sister who crushed on Greg for ages! We both had the best moment of our lives that night all thanks to Susie."

"Fast forward 30 years, Susie was also a well-known philanthropist because she helped so many great causes in our community, it would be hard to name them all. I know from personal experience because she helped me with one of the greatest challenges of my life. I was trying to put together a fundraiser/celebration for the Brevard Humane Society's 60th anniversary. Susie not only opened her 'little black book' of special names and addresses to send out invites, but she also helped me create what would become the very successful and well known 'Tuxes & Tails' gala, now and its 14th year! Not only did this event bring hundreds of thousands of dollars over the years for the Humane Society, but she also introduced me to Stacey, the 'drama mama' Executive Director of the Cocoa Village Playhouse. This partnership between the two organizations still brings much success for both groups to this day, all thanks to Susie! The most interesting part of all of this is the fact that Susie never had any pets and was not a real pet person. Her son, Drew, said he was surprised I had gotten her to help with the animals because she would never let him have a pet growing up. It was just her nature to want to help her friends and the community. The Humane Society and the Cocoa Village Playhouse continue to be blessed from her talents to this day, as well as Stacey and I are lifelong friends thanks to Susie's generosity."

Suzy Fleming Leonard was a staff member of *Florida Today* until she recently retired. She covered many events staged by Susie as part of her fundraising and charitable activities. Her article sharing the news of Susie's illness is included in Appendix A of this book.

"In 2002, I accepted an invitation to attend the Apollo 13 Gala at Kennedy Space Center. The evening included an opportunity to meet Apollo 13 astronaut Jim Lovell and Hollywood greats Tom Hanks and Ron Howard. But the most memorable luminaries I got to know that night were Susie and Tom Wasdin."

"In my 25 years as a writer and editor with *Florida Today*, I got to know the Wasdins as generous philanthropists and avid supporters of our community. But it wasn't until 2012, when Connie and Bob Harvey moved to Cocoa Village, that I really got to know the Wasdins. My husband Steve and I became friends with the Harveys soon after they moved into the condo next door to Tom and Susie, and it didn't take long for all of us to be pulled into the Wasdin world of giving back."

"Whether Connie and I were helping Susie plan an elaborate fundraiser for the Cocoa Village Playhouse, or we were gathering for Christmas Eve or the Fourth of July, I quickly learned that Susie was a larger-than-life hostess. No celebration was complete without an outlandish stunt. Corvette parade? Sure, why not. Living, breathing horses for photo ops at a Kentucky Derby party? Yep, she arranged that. Helicopter landing in Riverside Park or on the golf course at Rockledge Country Club? She made that happen, too."

"My favorite, though, was the night Tom and Susie's guests gathered around the baby grand piano in their living room for a sing-along as Songwriters Hall of Fame inductee Tony Macaulay played his hits: *Build Me Up Butter Cup, Love Grows, Last Night I Didn't Get to Sleep, Don't Give Up On Us,* and *Baby, Now That I've Found You.*"

"Glamor should be Susie's middle name. I've never seen her without sequins or rhinestones, even when she was headed to the gym. But in the midst of all that glitz, she still loved a good fart joke."

"Our community is certainly better for having Susie and Tom be a part of it, and my life is better for having known them."

Rita Moreno: Rita Moreno is the wife of Ruben Moreno, a prominent dermatologist in Brevard County and a frequent cast member in the productions of the Cocoa Village Playhouse. The Morenos are major contributors to various civic and charitable organizations in Brevard County.

"Susie Wasdin is a unique person and when she sees you,

she made you feel like you were the only person in the room. She was always interested in what you were doing, and she was always happy and full of life."

"She dedicated herself to many meaningful causes and spent a good part of her time fundraising in Brevard County. I especially loved her dedication to our Historic Cocoa Village Playhouse, a theatre that is near and dear to my heart."

"She was larger than life, a happy spirit, and a lovely lady."

These are just a few of the memories of Susie Wasdin shared by her friends. All of them carry the same message, Susie was a glamorous, funny, caring, and generous person who never met a stranger and who never made an enemy.

APPENDICES

APPENDIX A

FLORIDA TODAY
September 17-18, 2023

Living with Alzheimer's: Longtime Cocoa
philanthropist's light dims as the disease sets in

Suzy Fleming Leonard

A polished, black baby grand piano occupies a place of honor in a corner of the living room in Susie and Tom Wasdin's condo in Cocoa Village.

Behind it, a sliding glass door offers a panoramic view of the Indian River.

A few years ago, at one of the Wasdin's many parties, Tony Macaulay sat at the piano and played a sing-along of his hits, which include "Baby, Now That I've Found You," "Build Me Up Buttercup," and "(Last Night" I Didn't Get to Sleep at All."

These days, the piano mostly sits quiet unless Susie feels up to striking a few chords and arpeggios.

"She still plays the piano," Tom said. "She's concerned she's not playing it real well, but it sounds good to me."

Susie Wasdin, 74, has Alzheimer's disease.

Once a vibrant, glittering part of the Space Coast social scene who raised the millions of dollars for local organizations, she now spends her days in quiet contentment, sitting in a backroom of the condo with Tom watching sports on TV.

"We have a rule. Susie gets to do what Susie wants to do," said Tom, 88.

And one thing he knows Susie would want to do is to tell her story.

It's what she encouraged him to do back in 2008, when he went public with his struggles caused by trigeminal neuralgia, a condition that causes so much nerve pain the doctors sometimes call it "suicide pain," as some patients end up taking their own lives.

The Wasdins hoped that telling his story would help others suffering from the rare disease.

Now it's time to help others with Susie's story.

"Even in the position she's in now, she still wants to give," Tom said.

A quick decline

For more than three decades, Tom and Susie Wasdin were a power couple in Brevard. She helped him run Wasdin Associates, a real estate and rental company. They hosted lavish parties in their condo.

Susie planned fundraising events for non-profits, arts groups, political campaigns and education foundations.

They were always on the go.

She started showing slight signs of memory loss as early as 2017, Tom said

"I remember the first time she said to me, 'What's their names?'" he said. "She knew everybody. She worked the room. She knew everybody's name. I had to ask her people's names."

After that, she experienced a gradual, but consistent, decline in memory.

She started seeing a neurologist around 2018 and was

diagnosed with the beginning stages of Alzheimer's, he said.

The disease didn't become pronounced until the COVID-19 pandemic.

"The pandemic shut down her social life," Tom said. "She didn't get to see any of her friends. In my opinion it contributed to her rapid decline."

She's in the early stages of a clinical trial, he said, but it's too early to know if it's making a difference.

An all too common story

The Wasdins are hardly alone.

The numbers illuminating the effect of Alzheimer's disease and other dementias are staggering.

More than six million Americans—estimated 17,600 on the Space Coast alone—are living with Alzheimer's disease. According to the Alzheimer's Association, 1 in 3 seniors dies with Alzheimer's or another dementia such as vascular, Lewy body and frontotemporal dementia.

This year alone the cost of those diseases is estimated at $345 billion. That number is projected to rise to nearly $1 trillion in 2050, the year the youngest baby boomers, those born in 1965, turn that 85.

And dementia related numbers are rising in Florida said Lindsey Taylor, program manager for the Central and North Florida chapter of the Alzheimer's Association.

In 2020, 580,000 Floridians 65 and older had Alzheimer's figures show, Taylor said. By 2025, that number is expected to be 720,000.

"That's an almost 25% increase," she said. "And unfortunately, it is going to get worse before it gets better, if it does get better, because of how the population is aging."

That's why events such as the Walk to End Alzheimer's,

and year-round support for research and services for patients, families and caregivers, are so critical, she said.

The Walk to End Alzheimer's is held annually in more than 600 communities nationwide for the purpose of raising awareness and money for Alzheimer's care support and research. Brevard Walk to End Alzheimer's starts at 9:00 a.m. Sept. 23 at Riverfront Park in Cocoa Village, not far from the Wasdins' home.

An enduring love story

Tom loves looking back on their life before Alzheimer's.

"How did we meet" Susie said to Tom on a recent summer afternoon. They sat side-by-side on a leather reclining sofa sipping their lunchtime smoothies.

"It's been a long time ago, honey," he said. Cocoa Beach High School. I was the basketball coach, and you were involved in everything."

She smiled and nodded. She likes to hear stories about their adventures together, Tom said.

She was a popular majorette, cheerleader and homecoming queen, Cocoa Beach High School class of 1967.

"I didn't know her well, but I didn't like girls getting involved with my basketball program," he said. "You can't coach a lovesick player."

It would be 15 years before their paths crossed again.

Tom left Cocoa Beach after a couple of years and moved on to coach at Jacksonville University. Susie went to Brevard Junior College and University of Florida, where she earned a degree in education. She moved to Atlanta to teach.

In 1974, Tom gave up coaching and moved back to the Space Coast. While in Jacksonville, he'd spent summers managing the Canaveral Pier (now the Cocoa Beach Pier), which gave him the connections to launch a career in real estate development.

Susie returned to Brevard in the early 1980s. She was divorced with a 2-year-old son.

"She was looking for a job," Tom said. "Her mother told her to go talk to Coach Wasdin. I hired her on the spot"

Her assignment was pre-selling condos at Harbor Woods on Merritt Island.

"She sold 100 units in two days," Tom said.

In 1985, the couple got married at sunset on a sailboat right off Mallory square in Key West.

It was romantic, he said, and a bit of a happy surprise for him.

"Susie played a little trick on me," Tom said. "We'd talked about getting married sometime. We went to Key West for the weekend, and she showed me the wedding announcement she'd already mailed to all our friends."

He hasn't regretted making an honest woman of her.

A life of giving

The Wasdins quickly built a reputation for being philanthropic powerhouses.

Loved one-upping herself with each event she planned.

She brought in a horse so guests at a Kentucky Derby party pose for photos.

She arranged for the Cape Canaveral Corvette club to drive partygoers around town in a mini-parade.

At an event for the Brevard Humane Society, she charged attendees a premium to walk the red carpet with their pets.

At a party for the Historic Cocoa Village Playhouse, she had a helicopter land in Cocoa Village's Riverfront Park, an homage to an upcoming production of "Miss Saigon."

"Words cannot express what words cannot express," said Dr. Anastasia Hawkins-Smith, chief executive officer for the playhouse. "Susie Wasdin is one of the most special and kind beings I have ever known. To know her is the love her."

Hawkins Smith worked with Susie for more than 35 years on the Brevard Community College foundation.

"There were two things that immediately struck me: her energy and her absolute love for 'Coach' Tom," Hawkins-Smith said. "She is truly a force of nature. Beautiful, smart and absolutely everywhere. She and Tom were the dream team of philanthropy in the area and so giving of their time and talents."

Theresa Clifton, executive director of the Brevard Humane Society, is awed by Susie's willingness to raise money for animals, even though she's never owned, or even considered, getting a pet.

"It was quite a special moment one day 12 years ago when I asked her to help me with the celebration for the 60th anniversary of the Brevard Humane Society," Clifton said.

"I wanted to recognize the achievement in a big way and that was always her specialty, as she is a master of event planning especially on a shoestring budget. She opened her little black book and the Tuxes & Tails Gala was born. It was meant to be a one-time event, but she was so enthused with it, we had an overwhelming turnout. The much-needed funds that accompanied the almost 300 attendees sealed the deal for future Tuxes & Tails Galas."

The Humane Society recently hosted Its 12th annual Tuxes & Tails Gala.

Susie was on the eastern Florida State college foundation board from 2012-18, said Tonya Cherry, foundation executive director, and was heavily involved in fundraising for the EFSC foundation. Tom served on the board from 1996-03.

The Tom and Susie Wasdin Endowed Scholarship Fund supports Brevard County students enrolled in the bachelor's program at EFSC. It provides three $2,000 scholarships per academic year.

The Distinguished Alumni and Friends Scholarship supports Brevard County students with financial need who are pursuing a bachelor's degree. This scholarship was spearheaded by Susie, but has multiple donors. She is instrumental in keeping the account funded by reaching out to past Distinguished Alumni and friends of the college. The $1,000 award usually goes to two to four students per academic year.

These are just a sampling of the organizations Susie helped.

"It's a fact that the Playhouse — and the community as a whole for that matter—would not be the same without all of her work Hawkins-Smith said.

A day in the life of Alzheimer's

"She still likes to help people," Tom said of his wife.

"If he ask her to do something, she may or may not comply, but if he says "Susie will you help me by doing this?" she's always willing.

Her days are simple.

"She likes to smile. She likes to get dressed up in her nice outfits and go out to dinner," Tom said. "While we're at dinner, she enjoys having people come by and speak to her. She may not remember their names, but she enjoys it."

Health aides come in seven days a week, arriving in the morning and staying until dinner time. Tom knows he's lucky to be able to provide care for her in their home.

"I'm happy to be able to do what I'm doing" he said. "The goal is to keep her happy."

He sees it as an honor to look after his wife

"I'll ask her honey what do you want to do today," he said. "She'll say I don't care, as long as I'm with you."

Being a caregiver can get lonely, and Tom tries to maintain connections outside the world he and Susie now occupy. He attends a weekly support group meeting. He has breakfast with friends most week days. He takes Susie out for dinner, and on Fridays, they attend a weekly porch party at the riverfront home of friends.

"If I'd known it was going to turn out like this, I'd have still done it," he said. "Nothing makes me happier than to see her smile."

Their granddaughter, Delaney Stroh, is one of the aides who comes in regularly. Tom helped Delaney get Susie into a wheelchair and watched as the two headed down the hallway to get ready for Susie's afternoon nap.

"I love you, baby," he said as Delaney rolled her out of the room.

"I love you, too," Susie said, giving him a bright smile and a wave.

"Go have a good rest," he said gently, "and after you wake up we'll get dressed and go out to dinner."

The one thing Tom would do differently, given the chance, is to have appreciated what he had sooner.

"We've had a wonderful life," he said. "I just didn't realize it. Every morning I count my blessings, and we've had many."

"One morning, she asked me, 'Why did God let this happen to me?' I said I don't know, but I don't know why we had so many blessings, either."

APPENDIX B

SOCIAL SECURITY BENEFITS FOR ALZHEIMER'S PATIENTS

Individuals diagnosed with Alzheimer's disease, particularly early-onset Alzheimer's, may be eligible for Social Security disability benefits.

Here's how Social Security handles Alzheimer's disability claims:

1. Compassionate Allowances (CAL) Initiative:
   - Early-onset Alzheimer's disease is recognized under the SSA's Compassionate Allowances program.
   - This initiative fast-tracks the disability determination process for conditions deemed particularly severe, allowing for quicker access to benefits like Social Security Disability Insurance (SSDI) and Supplemental Security Income (SSI).

2. Qualifying for Benefits:
   - Meeting the SSA's Definition of Disability: To qualify, individuals with Alzheimer's must demonstrate a significant decline in cognitive abilities that prevents them from engaging in substantial gainful activity (SGA).
   - Medical Evidence: You'll need to provide medical documentation, including:

- Diagnosis of early-onset Alzheimer's.
- Proof of progressive decline in function or test scores over time.
- Details about your cognitive impairments and how they impact daily living and work.
- Results from relevant medical tests, such as neuropsychological testing.
- SSDI vs. SSI:
  - SSDI: For individuals who have worked and paid into Social Security taxes.
  - SSI: A needs-based program for individuals with limited income and resources.

3. Application Process:
   - Applying: You can apply online, in person, or by phone.
   - Required Information: You'll need to provide personal details, work history, and comprehensive medical information.
   - Importance of Medical Records: The SSA will carefully review your medical records to assess the severity of your Alzheimer's and its impact on your ability to work.

Important Notes:
   - Consulting with Professionals: Consider seeking assistance from a disability attorney or advocate who can guide you through the application process and help present your case effectively.
   - Do Not Delay: If you are diagnosed with early-onset Alzheimer's and are unable to work, don't delay applying for benefits, as waiting may result in a loss of substantial benefits.

- Appealing a Denial: If your initial claim is denied, don't be discouraged. Most initial claims are denied, and you have the right to appeal the decision.

Remember, while early-onset Alzheimer's may qualify for expedited processing, eligibility for disability benefits still depends on individual circumstances and demonstrating a severe enough condition to prevent work.

This is for informational purposes only. For medical advice or diagnosis, consult a professional.

APPENDIX C

ASSISTANCE OFFERED BY THE DEPARTMENT OF VETERANS AFFAIRS

The Department of Veterans Affairs (VA) provides a comprehensive range of services and benefits to support Veterans diagnosed with Alzheimer's disease or other forms of dementia.

Healthcare Services:
- Home-based primary care: A VA health care team provides services like nursing care and physical therapy in the Veteran's home.
- Homemaker/home health aide services: Trained caregivers offer assistance with daily living activities (ADLs) such as bathing, dressing, and meal preparation.
- Skilled home health care: Community-based home health agencies provide medical care like wound care, physical therapy, and social work support at home.
- Respite care: Short-term care options (in-home, adult day health care, or nursing home) provide temporary relief for caregivers.
- Adult day health care: A program for social activities, companionship, recreation, and assistance with ADLs.
- Outpatient and inpatient clinical care: Veterans can access various medical services at VA facilities.
- Nursing home care: The VA offers or contracts with

nursing homes, including Community Living Centers (CLCs) and State Veterans Homes, for full-time care with skilled nursing and help with ADLs.
- Palliative care: Focuses on pain and symptom management to enhance quality of life.
- Hospice care: Provided to Veterans with terminal illnesses to ensure comfort and support.

Financial Benefits:
- VA Pension: Provides supplemental monthly payments to qualifying wartime Veterans with limited income and assets.
- Aid & Attendance (A&A) benefit: An increased pension for Veterans or surviving spouses who require assistance with ADLs, often used to help cover long-term care costs.
- VA Survivors Pension: Provides financial support to eligible surviving spouses of wartime Veterans.
- VA disability benefits: Veterans whose dementia or Alzheimer's is linked to their military service may be eligible for monthly tax-free payments, with ratings ranging from 0% to 100% based on severity.

Caregiver Support:
- Program of Comprehensive Assistance for Family Caregivers (PCAFC): Provides support to eligible caregivers, including a monthly stipend, health care benefits, mental health counseling, respite care, and training.
- Program of General Caregiver Support Services (PGCSS): Offers various resources like skills training, coaching, support groups, and referrals.

- VA Caregiver Support Line: Provides information and assistance for caregivers at 1-855-260-3274.

Other Resources:
- Geriatric Research Education and Clinical Centers (GRECCs): Focused on research, innovation, and education to improve the health of aging Veterans.
- Home Improvements/Structural Alterations (HISA) program: Provides grants for home modifications to address mobility issues.
- Veteran Directed Care (VDC): Allows Veterans and caregivers to manage a budget for in-home care services and related needs.

Eligibility:
- Eligibility for VA services and benefits for Alzheimer's patients depends on various factors, including the Veteran's service history, health status, and financial situation.
- Contacting a VA social worker or the VA Caregiver Support Line is recommended for determining specific program eligibility and accessing services.

APPENDIX D

ASSISTANCE AVAILABLE FROM THE STATE OF FLORIDA

What assistance is available from the State of Florida for Alzheimer's patients?

The State of Florida, primarily through the Florida Department of Elder Affairs (DOEA), offers a variety of assistance programs and initiatives aimed at supporting individuals with Alzheimer's disease and related dementias (ADRD) and their caregivers.

Here are some key areas of assistance:

1. Alzheimer's Disease Initiative (ADI):
   - Respite Care Services: ADI offers temporary relief for caregivers of individuals with probable ADRD who have cognitive impairments impacting daily living. This includes in-home care, facility-based care, specialized adult day care, emergency respite care, and extended care up to 30 days.
   - Caregiver Support: Caregivers can access case management, specialized medical equipment and supplies, counseling and support groups, caregiver training, and relief services. These services are delivered through the state's 11 Area Agencies on Aging (AAAs).
   - Memory Disorder Clinics: The state has authorized

17 Memory Disorder Clinics (MDCs) in 13 service areas, providing comprehensive diagnostic and referral services, service-related research, caregiver training materials, and educational opportunities.

- State of Florida Brain Bank: This program coordinates brain tissue donations for research to advance understanding, diagnosis, and treatment of ADRD.

2. Florida Alzheimer's Center of Excellence (FACE):
   - This state-administered program supports caregivers and individuals with Alzheimer's and related dementias using evidence-based strategies.
   - FACE aims to achieve a holistic care model to help individuals with ADRD age-in-place and empower caregivers.
   - Care Navigators are available through FACE to connect individuals to resources and support. You can reach them by calling the Elder Helpline at 1-800-96-ELDER (1-800-963-5337).

3. Dementia Care and Cure Initiative (DCCI):
   - DCCI aims to promote dementia care, support research, and engage communities in Florida.

4. Additional Caregiver Assistance Programs:
   - Florida offers caregiver assistance through various programs, including Community Care For the Elderly (CCE), Home Care for the Elderly (HCE), National Family Caregiver Support Program, Respite for Elders Living in Everyday Families (RELIEF), and the Statewide Medicaid Managed Care Long-Term Care Program.

5. Therapeutic Robotic Pets and MP3 Players:
   - These resources are provided to socially isolated seniors and adults with ADRD to help with social isolation and depression.

To learn more about eligibility and access these services, you can:
- Contact your local Area Agency on Aging (AAA).
- Call the Elder Helpline at 1-800-96-ELDER (1-800-963-5337).
- Visit the Florida Department of Elder Affairs website for more information.

Note: The Alzheimer's Association is a national resource that partners with the Florida Department of Elder Affairs. You can visit their website or call their 24/7 Helpline at 800-272-3900 for additional support.

APPENDIX E

ALZHEIMER'S SUPPORT GROUPS IN FLORIDA

You can find a variety of Alzheimer's support groups in Florida, primarily through the Alzheimer's Association and other organizations dedicated to dementia care.

1. Alzheimer's Association Support Groups:
   - Florida Gulf Coast Chapter: Offers local support groups in 16 counties, serving caregivers and individuals with Alzheimer's and other dementias. These are offered via phone, video, or in person, and all services are free.
   - Central and North Florida Chapter: Supports 43 counties in this region with local support groups led by trained facilitators, available in person, via phone, or video.
   - Southeast Florida Chapter: Provides support groups in the eight counties of southeast Florida for caregivers and individuals living with Alzheimer's and dementia. They offer in-person and virtual options, including multilingual support groups.
   - ALZConnected® Online Community: A free online platform for people living with dementia

and their caregivers to connect, share experiences, and support each other.
- 24/7 Helpline: The Alzheimer's Association offers a free 24/7 Helpline at 800.272.3900 to provide confidential emotional support, crisis assistance, local resources, and information in over 200 languages.

2. Other Organizations and Specific Support Groups:
   - Alzheimer's and Dementia Resource Center (ADRC) – Central Florida: Provides facilitated support groups for caregivers in the central Florida area. They offer in-person and virtual options, including groups for Spanish-speaking caregivers and a "Men's Breakfast Club."
   - The Dubin Center – Fort Myers: Offers various support groups for caregivers, including general caregiver, men's, grief, early-stage, and frontotemporal dementia (FTD) groups.
   - USF Health's Alzheimer's Caregiver Support Groups – Tampa: The Byrd Alzheimer's Institute offers free virtual caregiver support groups.
   - Brevard Alzheimer's Foundation – Melbourne: Offers in-person caregiver support groups at the Center for Family Caregivers, including caregiver-to-caregiver and caring for the caregiver groups.
   - Alzheimer's Community Care – Palm Beach, Martin, and St. Lucie County: Leads caregiver support groups in these counties, offering information, guidance from licensed nurses, and support from active caregivers.

- Dementia Spotlight Foundation – Brooksville: Hosts a caregiver support group to connect with others facing similar challenges and gain helpful tips.

Types of Support Groups Available:
- Early-stage support groups: Designed for individuals with a physician's diagnosis of Alzheimer's or other dementia, providing a safe environment to discuss their diagnosis and symptoms.
- Caregiver support groups: Offer comfort, reassurance, and practical advice to unpaid family members or friends caring for someone with Alzheimer's or related disorders.
- Specialized support groups: Some organizations offer groups focused on specific needs, such as grief support, men's groups, or groups for adult daughters and granddaughters.

Note: Always verify the support group details, including dates, times, and locations, by contacting the listed organization before attending.

APPENDIX F

PRIVATE FOUNDATIONS AID AND ASSISTANCE GRANTS IN FLORIDA

There are private foundations and grants available for Alzheimer's patients in Florida.

Private Foundations & Grants:
- The Carl Angus DeSantis Foundation: This foundation supports programs and organizations focused on improving human health, including Alzheimer's disease research and care.
- Florida Atlantic University (FAU): FAU received a $750,000 grant from the Carl Angus DeSantis Foundation to establish best practices for coordinated care and research for Alzheimer's disease and related dementias.
- Alzheimer's Foundation of America (AFA):
- Anne & Irving Brodsky Innovation Grant: This grant provides $25,000 for innovative programs that improve the lives of individuals with Alzheimer's and their families.
- Bi-Annual Grant: This grant provides $6,000 twice a year for programs and services that support individuals, families, and caregivers affected by Alzheimer's disease and related dementias.
- Foundations in Sanford, Florida: Several foundations

in Sanford, Florida provide grants specifically for Alzheimer's disease research and support, including the Central Florida Auto Dealers Association Inc. and the Tracy Forrest Foundation Inc.

- Alzheimer's Association: Offers the Center for Dementia Respite Innovation (CDRI) start-up awards ($50,000 per year for two years) to organizations and providers who want to launch dementia-specific respite programs.
- Note: Some grants are intended for organizations or researchers to develop and implement programs and services, while others directly benefit individuals and families. Alzheimer's Foundation of America and the Florida Department of Health websites offer more detailed information about their grant programs and application processes. You can also explore resources like Instrumentl to find information on foundations in specific areas of Florida that are funding Alzheimer's disease initiatives.
- Reach out to local Area Agencies on Aging or memory clinics in Florida.
- Explore the resources offered by the Alzheimer's Association, including their BenefitsCheckUp tool.

APPENDIX G

SUPPORT FOR VETERANS WITH ALZHEIMER'S/DEMENTIA

- A range of VA health care services: This includes services such as Home Based Primary Care, Homemaker and Home Health Aide, Respite Care, Adult Day Health Care, outpatient and inpatient hospital care, nursing home care, palliative care, and hospice care.
- Memory care benefits and programs: The VA offers various health benefits, pensions, and disability benefits to help cover the costs of memory care facilities and other dementia-related care.
- Veteran Directed Care (VDC) program: This program allows veterans to manage a budget for care services and select their preferred care providers, potentially including family members.
- Disability compensation: Veterans with Alzheimer's or dementia may be eligible for monthly, tax-free disability payments if their condition is service-connected or was worsened by their service.

For Caregivers of Veterans with Alzheimer's/Dementia:
- Caregiver Support Program: This program offers clinical services, resources, and support for caregivers of eligible veterans, including monthly stipends, health insurance access, mental health counseling, respite care, and training.

- REACH VA program: This program provides coaching and support to help caregivers manage stress, learn new skills, and improve their ability to care for veterans with dementia, among other conditions.
- Dementia Caregiver Support resources: The VA website provides information and resources on managing difficult behaviors, safety, and support for in-home care.
- VA Caregiver Support Line: You can call 1-855-260-3274 for information, support, and assistance connecting with local VA resources.

To learn more and access these services:
- Visit the VA website on Dementia Care (including Alzheimer's Disease).
- Contact your local VA Medical Center or VA social worker.
- Call the VA Caregiver Support Line at 1-855-260-3274.

This is for informational purposes only. For medical advice or diagnosis, consult a professional. AI responses may include mistakes.

APPENDIX H

NEW BLOOD TEST FOR DETERMINING ALZHEIMER'S

- The U.S. Food and Drug Administration (FDA) has cleared the Lumipulse G pTau217/ß-Amyloid 1-42 Plasma Ratio as the first blood test to aid in the diagnosis of Alzheimer's disease.
- This test is designed for individuals aged 55 and older who are exhibiting signs and symptoms of Alzheimer's disease.
- It works by analyzing the ratio of two key proteins, pTau217 and beta-amyloid 1-42, in the blood plasma.
- An elevated ratio of these proteins correlates to the presence of amyloid plaques in the brain, a hallmark of Alzheimer's.

How it fits into the diagnostic process:
- The blood test is not intended as a stand-alone diagnostic tool.
- It should be used as part of a larger diagnostic process, which includes a clinical evaluation by a doctor to assess cognitive function and rule out other potential causes of memory problems.
- If the blood test results are positive, indicating a high likelihood of amyloid plaques, further testing, such as a PET scan or spinal tap (lumbar puncture), may be needed to confirm the diagnosis.

Benefits of the blood test:
- Less invasive: Compared to traditional diagnostic methods like PET scans or spinal taps, a simple blood draw is less invasive and more comfortable for patients.
- Potential for earlier detection: The test can help detect the presence of amyloid plaques, which can accumulate in the brain years before symptoms appear, potentially leading to earlier diagnosis and intervention.
- Reduced cost: Blood tests are generally less expensive than PET scans or spinal taps.
- Increased accessibility: Blood tests can be more readily available, potentially expanding access to Alzheimer's diagnosis.

Important Considerations:
- Not a definitive diagnosis: A positive blood test result suggests a high likelihood of Alzheimer's-related pathology, but it is not a definitive diagnosis on its own.
- Requires interpretation by specialists: Results should be interpreted by Alzheimer's specialists in conjunction with other clinical information.
- False positives and negatives are possible: While the Lumipulse test has shown high accuracy (around 92% for positive results, 97% for negative results), false positive and false negative results can occur.
- Insurance coverage: While expected to be covered by insurance, including Medicare, this is a developing area.

In summary, the development of blood tests for Alzheimer's disease, like the FDA-cleared Lumipulse G pTau217/ß-Amyloid 1-42 Plasma Ratio, is a significant advancement that offers a less invasive, potentially earlier, and more accessible option to aid in the diagnostic process for eligible individuals.

www.ingramcontent.com/pod-product-compliance
Lightning Source LLC
Chambersburg PA
CBHW031851090426
42741CB00005B/444